The Divine Art of Living

Selections from Writings of
Bahá'u'lláh and 'Abdu'l-Bahá

COMPILED

by

MABEL HYDE PAINE

BAHÁ'Í PUBLISHING TRUST

WILMETTE, ILLINOIS

Revised edition 1960
Fourth printing 1973

ISBN: 0–87743–017–9 (cloth)
ISBN: 0–87743–005–5 (paper)
Library of Congress Catalog Card No.: 44–9844

CONTENTS

THE DIVINE ART OF LIVING

A Compilation

PREFACE

"Thy Word is a light unto my path and a lamp unto my feet," sang the Psalmist. Jesus Christ spoke of Himself and His Teachings as "The Way, the Truth, and the Life," and said: "The words that I speak . . . are spirit and life." Buddha taught His followers the *"Eightfold Path."* The great preoccupation of all the Messengers of God has been to guide mankind along the pathway to real life and truth. For this They have lived and suffered and given mankind words of Divine counsel and inspiration. The Guardian of the Bahá'í Faith, Shoghi Effendi, assures us that progress along the line of spiritual development is endless. 'Abdu'l-Bahá called the *"Highway of the Kingdom," "a straight and far-stretching path."* It is a glorious path to follow.

Such thoughts as these led the editors of *World Order*, the Bahá'í Magazine, to arrange for a compilation on the "Divine Art of Living" to appear in successive numbers of that magazine from April, 1940 through September, 1941. This book is a revision of the compilation which appeared in the magazine. The limitations of space in the magazine had tended to make the treatment deficient in some ways, and it was felt that a revision would better fulfill the original purpose.

The title is borrowed from a previous compilation having the same aim and same general character, which was made by Mrs. Mary M. Rabb. Mrs. Rabb's book was much loved by many readers. She has kindly consented to the use of her title in this compilation. This is, however, a completely new compilation.

The sources of the compilation are, mainly, the written words of Bahá'u'lláh, the Founder of the Bahá'í Faith, and the written words and public addresses of 'Abdu'l-Bahá, the Interpreter of that Faith. In a few instances, where the source seemed reliable, reported words of 'Abdu'l-Bahá have been used. There are also a few selections from the New Testament. As Bahá'u'lláh and 'Abdu'l-Bahá both presented the Bahá'í Teachings to the Western world as the carrying on and fulfillment of the Message of Christ it seemed fitting to include some passages from the New Testament, especially as this book will be read by those who have grown up in the Christian Faith.

The chapters of the book treat of outstanding qualities which characterize holy living, goals along the shining pathway of the Kingdom. The words of Bahá'u'lláh and 'Abdu'l-Bahá on this all-absorbing subject fill many volumes. It is hoped that these chapters of selections will stimulate the reader to search these scriptures himself and thus drink deep of the very Water of Life.

M. H. PAINE

Urbana, Illinois

Editorial Note: The 1960 edition of *The Divine Art of Living* represents a few revisions to exclude some selections from the reported sayings of 'Abdu'l-Bahá or to replace an old translation with a new, as for example, *The Secret of Divine Civilization*. In some instances selections remaining in this compilation do not always represent the exact rendering of current translations although the variance is slight. For a completely accurate rendition of any passage, the original work cited in the Reference Notes should be used.

CHAPTER ONE

TRUST IN GOD

ARE not five sparrows sold for two farthings, and not one of them is forgotten before God?

But even the very hairs of your head are all numbered. Fear not, therefore; ye are of more value than many sparrows.   1

O trust in God! for His bounty is everlasting, and in His blessings for they are superb. O put your faith in the Almighty, for He faileth not and His goodness endureth forever! His Sun giveth light continually, and the clouds of His mercy are full of the waters of compassion with which He waters the hearts of all who trust in Him. His refreshing breeze ever carries healing in its wings to the parched souls of men.   2

Do not look at thy weakness; nay look at the power of thy Lord, which hath surrounded all regions.   3

Trust in the assistance of thy Master, and ask what thou wishest of the gifts of Thy Lord, the Unconstrained.   4

If thou art seeking after spiritual tranquillity, turn thy face at all times toward the Kingdom of Abhá* . . . Let not thy hands tremble nor thy heart be disturbed, but rather be confident and firm in the love of thy Lord, the Merciful, the Clement.   5, 6

Trust in God, and be unmoved by either praise or false accusations . . . depend entirely on God.   7

In all thine affairs put thy reliance in God, and commit them unto Him.   8

---

* Abhá, literally, The Most Glorious

The source of all good is trust in God, submission unto His command, and contentment in His holy will and pleasure.　　9

TRUST WHEN IN DIFFICULTIES

Today, humanity is bowed down with trouble, sorrow and grief, no one escapes; the world is wet with tears; but, thank God, the remedy is at our doors. Let us turn our hearts away from the world of matter and live in the spiritual world. It alone can give us freedom. If we are hemmed in by difficulties we have only to call upon God, and by His great mercy we shall be helped.

If sorrow and adversity visit us, let us turn our faces to the Kingdom and heavenly consolation will be outpoured.

If we are sick and in distress let us implore God's healing, and He will answer our prayer.

When our thoughts are filled with the bitterness of this world, let us turn our eyes to the sweetness of God's compassion and He will send us heavenly calm! If we are imprisoned in the material world, our spirit can soar into the Heavens and we shall be free indeed!

When our days are drawing to a close let us think of the eternal worlds, and we shall be full of joy!　　10

Be not in despair, but rather smile by the mercy of thy Lord; and be not sorrowful when meeting with worldly difficulties and depressions, for they pass away—and thine shall be immortality during ages and centuries, times and cycles.　　11

And when I am anxious . . . I anticipate the manifestations of Thy bounties from all sides!　　12

But thou must submit to and rely upon God under all conditions and He will bestow upon thee that which is conducive to thy well-being. Verily He is merciful and compassionate! For how many an affair was involved in difficulty and then was straightened, and how many a problem was solved by the permission of God.　　13

As to the subject of babes and infants and weak ones who are afflicted by the hands of oppressors: this contains great wisdom and this subject is of paramount importance. In brief, for those souls there is a recompense in another world and many details are connected with this matter. For those souls that suffering is the greatest mercy of God. Verily that mercy of the Lord is far better and preferable to all the comfort of this world and the growth and development of this place of mortality.   14

TRUST GOD RATHER THAN SELF

These events (such as the Titanic disaster) have deeper reasons. Their object is to teach man certain lessons. We are living in a day of reliance upon material conditions. Men imagine that the great size and strength of a ship, perfection of machinery or the skill of a navigator will insure safety, but these disasters sometimes take place that men may know that God is the real protector. If it be the will of God to protect man, a little ship may escape destruction whereas the greatest and most perfectly constructed vessel with the best and most skilful navigator may not survive a danger such as was present on the ocean. The purpose is that the people of the world may turn to God, the one Protector; that human souls may rely upon His preservation and know that He is the real safety. These events happen in order that man's faith may be increased and strengthened. Therefore, although we feel sad and disheartened, we must supplicate God to turn our hearts to the Kingdom, and pray for these departed souls with faith in His infinite mercy, so that although they have been deprived of this earthly life they may enjoy a new existence in the supreme mansions of the heavenly Father.

Let no one imagine that these words imply that man should not be thorough and careful in his undertakings. God has endowed man with intelligence so that he may safeguard and protect himself. Therefore he must provide and surround himself with all that scientific skill can produce. He must be deliberate, thoughtful and thorough in his purposes, build the best ship and provide the most experienced captain, yet withal let him rely upon God and consider God as the one keeper.   15

GRACE, FORGIVENESS AND MERCY OF GOD

Thou art He, O my God, through Whose names the sick are healed and the ailing are restored, and the thirsty are given drink, and the sore-vexed are tranquillized, and the wayward are guided, and the abased are exalted, and the poor are enriched, and the ignorant are enlightened, and the gloomy are illumined, and the sorrowful are cheered, and the chilled are warmed, and the downtrodden are raised up. Through Thy Name, O my God, all created things were stirred up, and the heavens were spread, and the earth was established, and the clouds were raised and made to rain upon the earth. This, verily, is a token of Thy grace unto all Thy creatures. 16

Every existence, whether seen or unseen, O my Lord, testifieth that Thy mercy hath surpassed all created things, and Thy loving-kindness embraced the entire creation. 17

Thou are the All-Bountiful, the overflowing showers of whose mercy have rained down upon high and low alike, and the splendors of whose grace have been shed over both the obedient and the rebellious. 18

Wash away, then, my sins, O my God, by Thy grace and bounty, and reckon me among such as are not overtaken by fear nor put to grief. 19

O Thou Who art the All-Knowing! Wayward though we be, we still cling to Thy bounty; and though ignorant, we still set our faces toward the ocean of Thy wisdom. Thou art that All-Bountiful Who art not deterred by a multitude of sins from vouchsafing Thy bounty, and the flow of Whose gifts is not arrested by the withdrawal of the peoples of the world. From eternity the door of Thy grace hath remained wide open. A dewdrop out of the ocean of Thy mercy is able to adorn all things with the ornament of sanctity, and a sprinkling of the waters of Thy bounty can cause the entire creation to attain unto true wealth. . . .

From eternity the tokens of Thy bounty have encompassed the universe, and the splendors of Thy Most Great Name have been shed over all created things. Deny not Thy servants the wonders of Thy grace. Cause them to be made aware of Thee, that they may bear witness to Thy unity, and enable them to recognize Thee, that they may hasten towards Thee. Thy mercy hath embraced the whole creation, and Thy grace hath pervaded all things. From the billows of the ocean of Thy generosity the seas of eagerness and enthusiasm were revealed. Thou art what Thou art. Aught except Thee is unworthy of any mention unless it entereth beneath Thy shadow, and gaineth admittance into Thy court.

Whatever betide us, we beseech Thine ancient forgiveness, and seek Thine all-pervasive grace.   20

TRUST IN GOD TO SEND HIS DIVINE MANIFESTATIONS*

We cannot say that the Divine bounty has ceased, that the glory of Divinity is exhausted or the Sun of Truth sunk into eternal sunset, into that night that is not followed by a sunrise and dawn, into that death which is not followed by life, into that error which is not followed by Truth. Is it conceivable that the Sun of Reality should sink into an eternal darkness? No! The sun was created in order that it may shed light upon the world and train all the kingdoms of existence. How then can the ideal Sun of Truth, the Word of God, set forever? For this would mean the cessation of the divine bounty, and the divine bounty by its very nature is continuous and ceaseless. Its sun is ever shining, its cloud is ever producing rain, its breezes are ever blowing, its bestowals are all-comprehending, its gifts are ever perfect. Consequently we must always anticipate, always be hopeful and pray to God that He will send unto us His Holy Manifestations* in their most perfect might, with the Divine penetrative power of His Word.   21

---

* i.e. great world prophets. "Manifestations" when spelled with a capital "M" signifies in these pages a divinely perfect master who manifests the attributes of God as a pure polished mirror reflects the sun.

CHAPTER TWO

ENTRANCE INTO THE KINGDOM OF GOD

SECOND BIRTH

EXCEPT a man be born again, he cannot see the Kingdom of God. . . .

Except a man be born of water and the Spirit, he cannot enter into the Kingdom of God. . . .

That which is born of the flesh is flesh; and that which is born of the Spirit is spirit.   1

There is . . . spirit which may be termed the divine, to which Jesus Christ refers when He declares that man must be born of its quickening and baptized with its living fire. Souls deprived of that spirit are accounted as dead, though they are possessed of the human spirit. His Holiness Jesus Christ has pronounced them dead inasmuch as they have no portion of the divine spirit. He says: "Let the dead bury their dead." In another instance He declares: "That which is born of the flesh is flesh; and that which is born of the spirit is spirit." By this He means that souls though alive in the human kingdom are nevertheless dead if devoid of this particular spirit of divine quickening. They have not partaken of the divine life of the higher kingdom; for the soul which partakes of the power of the divine spirit is verily living.   2

Know thou, verily, God hath preferred the insight to the sight; because the sight sees the material things, while the insight apprehends the spiritual. The former witnesses the earthly world, while the latter sees the world of the Kingdom. The former's judgment is temporary, while the latter's vision is everlasting. . . . 3

Entrance into the Kingdom is through the love of God, through detachment, through holiness and chastity, through truthfulness, purity, steadfastness, faithfulness, and the sacrifice of life. . . . For those who believe in God, who have love of God, and faith, life is excellent — that is, it is eternal; but to those souls who are veiled from God . . . it is dark . . .   4

May you be given life! . . .
Turn your faces away from the contemplation of your own finite selves and fix your eyes upon the Everlasting Radiance; then will your souls receive in full measure the divine power of the Spirit and the blessings of the Infinite Bounty.   5

HAPPINESS AND POWER

I was happy in imprisonment. I was in the utmost elation, for I was not a criminal, they had imprisoned me in the path of God. . . . I was happy that—praise be to God—I was a prisoner in the Cause of God, that my life was not wasted, that it was spent in the Divine service. Nobody who saw me imagined that I was in prison. They beheld me in the utmost joy, complete thankfulness and health, paying no attention to the prison.*   6

Happiness consists of two kinds; physical and spiritual. The physical happiness is limited; its utmost duration is one day, one month, one year. It hath no result. Spiritual happiness is eternal and unfathomable. This kind of happiness appeareth in one's soul with the love of God and suffereth one to attain to the virtues and perfections of the world of humanity. Therefore, endeavor as much as thou art able in order to illumine the lamp of thy heart by the light of love.
. . . Anybody can be happy in the state of comfort, ease, health, success, pleasure and joy; but if one will be happy and

---

* The prison in Palestine to which Bahá'u'lláh and His family and some Bahá'ís were sent in 1868.

contented in the time of trouble, hardship and prevailing disease, it is the proof of nobility. . . .

. . . If material anxiety envelopes you in a dark cloud, spiritual radiance lightens your path. Verily, those whose minds are illumined by the Spirit of the Most High have supreme consolation.

I myself was in prison forty years—one year alone would have been impossible to bear—nobody survived that imprisonment more than a year! But, thank God, during all those forty years I was supremely happy! Every day, on waking, it was like hearing good tidings, and every night infinite joy was mine. Spirituality was my comfort, and turning to God was my greatest joy. If this had not been so, do you think it possible that I could have lived through those forty years . . .

Thus, Spirituality is the greatest of God's gifts, and "Life Everlasting" means "Turning to God." May you, one and all, increase daily in spirituality, may you be strengthened in all goodness, may you be helped more and more by the Divine consolation, be made free by the Holy Spirit of God, and may the power of the Heavenly Kingdom live and work among you.   7

Then know, O thou virtuous soul, that as soon as thou becomest separated from aught else save God and dost cut thyself from the worldly things, thy heart will shine with the lights of divinity and with the effulgence of the Sun of Truth from the horizon of the Realm of Might, and then thou wilt be filled by the spirit of power from God and become capable of doing that which thou desirest. This is the confirmed truth.   8

When a man is thirsty he drinks water. When he is hungry he eats food. But if a man be not thirsty, water gives him no pleasure and if his hunger be already satisfied, food is distasteful to him.

This is not so with spiritual enjoyments. Spiritual enjoyments bring always joy. The love of God brings endless happiness. These are joys in themselves and not alleviations. The life of animals is more simple than that of man. Animals have all their needs supplied for them. All the grasses of the meadows are free to them. The birds build their nests in the branching trees and the palaces of kings are not so beautiful. If earthly needs are all, then the animals are better supplied than man. But man has another food, the heavenly manna of the knowledge of God. All the Divine prophets and Manifestations appeared in the world that this heavenly manna might be given to man. This is the food which fosters spiritual growth and strength and causes pure illumination in the souls of men. They become filled with the breaths of the Holy Spirit. They increase in the knowledge of God and those virtues which belong to the world of humanity. They attain to the very image and likeness of God.

God created in us a divine holy spirit—the human spirit with its intellectual powers which are above the powers of nature. By this we enjoy the ecstasies of the spirit and see the world illumined. The tree and the stone have not this power; they have no mind or soul; therefore they are excused. We are not excused. This power gives man effectual control over nature. He is enabled to discover reality and bring invisible things into the courts of the visible. Thus he is enabled to render effective the will of God and give it material station. This is what is meant by Bahá'u'lláh when He said, "Verily We have created you rich, why have ye made yourselves poor?" And Jesus Christ when He said, "The Father is in Me and I in you." It was this power which through Bahá'u'lláh said, "Noble have I created you, why do ye degrade yourselves?" This power distinguishes you above all other creatures, why do you devote it only to your material conditions? This is that which should be used for the acquisition and manifestation of the bounties of God, that ye may establish the Kingdom of God among men and attain to happiness in both worlds, the visible and the invisible.   9

Know thou that there are two kinds of happiness, spiritual and material.

As to material happiness, it never exists; nay, it is but imagination, an image reflected in mirrors, a specter and shadow. Consider the nature of material happiness. It is something which but slightly removes one's afflictions; yet the people imagine it to be joy, delight, exultation and blessing. All the material blessings, including food, drink, etc., tend only to allay thirst, hunger and fatigue. They bestow no delight on the mind nor pleasure on the soul; nay they furnish only the bodily wants. So this kind of happiness has no real existence.

As to spiritual happiness, this is the true basis of the life of man, for life is created for happiness, not for sorrow; for pleasure, not for grief. Happiness is life; sorrow is death. Spiritual happiness is life eternal. This is a light which is not followed by darkness. This is an honor which is not followed by shame. This is a life that is not followed by death. This is an existence that is not followed by annihilation. This great blessing and precious gift is obtained by man only through the guidance of God. . . .

This happiness is the fundamental basis from which man is created, worlds are originated, the contingent beings have existence and the world of God appears like unto the appearance of the sun at mid-day.

This happiness is but the love of God. . . .

Were it not for this happiness the world of existence would not have been created.   10

O Son of Man! Rejoice in the gladness of thine heart, that thou mayest be worthy to meet Me and to mirror forth My beauty. 11

This is the day of rejoicing and the hour of ecstasy! This is the season of the dead arising from the graves and gathering together! And this is the promised time for the attainment of plenteous grace.

Be calm, be strong, be grateful, and become a lamp full of light, that the darkness of sorrows be annihilated, and that the sun of everlasting joy arise from the dawning-place of heart and soul, shining brightly.   12

NEED OF CAPACITY

In the beginning of his human life man was embryonic in the world of the matrix. There he received capacity and endowment for the reality of human existence. The forces and powers necessary for this world were bestowed upon him in that limited condition. In this world he needed eyes; he received them potentially in the other. He needed ears; he obtained them there in readiness and preparation for his new existence. The powers requisite in this world were conferred upon him in the world of the matrix.

Therefore in this world he must prepare himself for the life beyond. That which he needs in the world of the Kingdom must be obtained here. Just as he prepared himself in the world of the matrix by acquiring forces necessary in this sphere of existence, so likewise the indispensable forces of the divine existence must be potentially obtained in this world.

What is he in need of in the Kingdom, which transcends the life and limitation of this mortal sphere? That world beyond is a world of sanctity and radiance; therefore it is necessary that in this world he should acquire these divine attributes. In that world there is need of spirituality, faith, assurance, the knowledge and love of God. These he must attain in this world so that after his ascension from the earthly to the heavenly Kingdom he shall find all that is needful in that life eternal ready for him.

That divine world is manifestly a world of lights; therefore man has need of illumination here. That is a world of love; the love of God is essential. It is a world of perfection; virtues or perfections must be acquired. That world is vivified by the breaths of the Holy Spirit; in this world we must seek them. That is the kingdom of life everlasting; it must be attained during this vanishing existence.

By what means can man acquire these things? How shall he obtain these merciful gifts and powers? First, through the knowledge of God. Second, through the love of God. Third, through faith. Fourth, through philanthropic deeds. Fifth, through self-sacrifice. Sixth, through severance from this world. Seventh, through sanctity and holiness. Unless he acquires these forces and attains to these requirements he will surely be deprived of the life that is eternal. But if he possesses the knowledge of God, becomes ignited through the fire of the love of God, becomes the cause of love among mankind, and lives in the utmost state af sanctity and holiness, he shall surely attain to second birth, be baptized by the Holy Spirit and enjoy everlasting existence. 13

A PRAYER BY 'ABDU'L-BAHÁ

O Thou the Compassionate God! Bestow upon me a heart which, like unto glass, may be illumined with the light of Thy love, and confer upon me a thought which may change this world into a rose-garden through the spiritual bounty. Thou art the Compassionate, the Merciful! Thou art the Great Beneficent God! 14

CHAPTER THREE

ADVANCING TOWARD THE IMMORTAL REALM

O SON of Love! Thou art but one step away from the glorious heights above and from the celestial tree of love. Take thou one pace and with the next advance into the immortal realm and enter the pavilion of eternity. Give ear then to that which hath been revealed by the Pen of Glory.　　1

O Son of Spirit! The best beloved of all things in My sight is Justice; turn not away therefrom if thou desirest Me, and neglect it not that I may confide in thee. By its aid thou shalt see with thine own eyes and not through the eyes of others, and shalt know of thine own knowledge and not through the knowledge of thy neighbor. Ponder this in thy heart; how it behoveth thee to be. Verily justice is My gift to thee and the sign of My lovingkindness. Set it then before thine eyes.　　2

Therefore it is our duty in this radiant century to investigate the essentials of Divine religion, seek the realities underlying the oneness of humanity and discover the source of fellowship and agreement which will unite mankind in the heavenly bond of love.　　3

I beg of God that the divine light which is spoken of in the Twelfth Chapter of John may shed its rays upon thee forever so that thou mayest always be in light. The life of man in this world is short and will soon draw to an end. Consequently one must appreciate (or count as gain) every breath (or moment) of his life and endeavor in that which is conducive to eternal glory.　　4

O Son of Being! Bring thyself to account each day ere thou art summoned to a reckoning; for death, unheralded, shall come upon thee, and thou shalt be called to give account for thy deeds.   5

A new life is, in this age, stirring within all the peoples of the earth; and yet none hath discovered its cause or perceived its motive. Consider the people of the West. Witness how, in their pursuit of that which is vain and trivial, they have sacrificed, and are still sacrificing, countless lives for the sake of its establishment and promotion. . . . O friends! Be not careless of the virtues with which ye have been endowed, neither be neglectful of your high destiny. Suffer not your labors to be wasted through the vain imaginations which certain hearts have devised.   6

.   . Happy are the wise that have recognized the straight path of God and turned unto His Kingdom; happy are the glad and sincere, the lamps of whose hearts burn with the knowledge of the All-Merciful and are protected by self-abnegation from the rough winds of tests and sorrows; happy are the brave whose hearts the power of the oppressor cannot daunt; happy are the clear-sighted that have learned to distinguish the transitory from the eternal, that have turned their faces to the Imperishable and are named among the Immortals in the realm of power and glory. . . .   7

. . . How excellent, how honorable is man if he arises to fulfil his responsibilities; how wretched and contemptible, if he shuts his eyes to the welfare of society and wastes his precious life in pursuing his own selfish interests and personal advantages. Supreme happiness is man's, and he beholds the signs of God in the world and in the human soul, if he urges on the steed of high endeavor in the arena of civilization and justice. . . .

. . . They have not properly understood that man's supreme honor and real happiness lie in self-respect, in high resolves and noble purposes, in integrity and moral quality, in immaculacy of mind. They have, rather, imagined that their greatness consists in the accumulation, by whatever means may offer, of worldly goods.

. . . How can he stain this immaculate garment with the filth of selfish desires, or exchange this everlasting honor for infamy? . . .

. . . The happiness and greatness, the rank and station, the pleasure and peace, of an individual have never consisted in his personal wealth, but rather in his excellent character, his high resolve, the breadth of his learning, and his ability to solve difficult problems. . . .   8

You ask if, through the appearance of the Kingdom of God, every soul hath been saved. The Sun of Reality hath appeared to all the world. This luminous appearance is salvation and life; but only he who hath opened the eye of reality and who hath seen these lights will be saved.   9

The Purpose of Our Lives

I bear witness, O my God, that Thou hast created me to know Thee and to worship Thee. I testify, at this moment, to my powerlessness and to Thy might, to my poverty and to Thy wealth.

There is none other God but Thee, the Help-in-Peril, the Self-Subsisting.   10

The purpose of God in creating man hath been, and will ever be, to enable him to know his Creator and to attain His Presence. To this most excellent aim, this supreme objective, all the heavenly Books and the divinely-revealed and weighty Scriptures unequivocally bear witness.   11

According to the words of the Old Testament, God has said, "Let us make man in Our image, after Our likeness." This indicates that man is of the image and likeness of God; that is to say, the perfections of God, the divine virtues are reflected or revealed in the human reality. Just as the light and effulgence of the sun when cast upon a polished mirror are reflected fully, gloriously, so likewise the qualities and attributes of divinity are radiated from the depths of a pure human heart. This is an evidence that man is the most noble of God's creatures. . . .

Let us now discover more specifically how he is the image and likeness of God and what is the standard or criterion by which he can be measured and estimated. This standard can be no other than the divine virtues which are revealed in him. Therefore every man imbued with divine qualities, who reflects heavenly moralities and perfections, who is the expression of ideal and praiseworthy attributes, is verily in the image and likeness of God.   12

Man is said to be the greatest representative of God, he is the Book of Creation because all the mysteries of being exist in him. If he comes under the shadow of the True Educator and is rightly trained, he becomes the essence of essences, the light of lights, the spirit of spirits; he becomes the center of the divine appearances, the source of spiritual qualities, the rising place of heavenly lights and the receptacle of divine inspirations. If he is deprived of this education he becomes the manifestation of satanic qualities, the sum of animal vices, and the source of all dark conditions.   13

O army of life! East and West have joined to worship stars of faded splendor and have turned in prayer unto darkened horizons. Both have utterly neglected the broad foundation of God's sacred laws, and have grown unmindful of the merits and virtues of His religion. They have regarded certain customs and conventions as the immutable basis of the Divine Faith, and have firmly established themselves therein. They have imagined themselves as having attained the glorious pinnacle of achievement and prosperity when in reality they have touched the innermost depths of heedlessness and deprived themselves wholly of God's bountiful gifts.

The corner-stone of the religion of God is the acquisition of the Divine perfections and the sharing in His manifold bestowals. The essential purpose of Faith and Belief is to ennoble the inner being of man with the outpourings of grace from on high. If this be not attained, it is indeed deprivation itself. It is the torment of infernal fire.

Wherefore it is incumbent upon all Bahá'ís to ponder this very delicate and vital matter in their hearts, that, unlike other religions, they may not content themselves with the noise, the clamor, the hollowness of religious doctrine. Nay, rather, they should exemplify in every aspect of their lives those attributes and virtues that are born of God and should arise to distinguish themselves by their goodly behavior. They should justify their claim to be Bahá'ís by deeds and not by name. He is a true Bahá'í who strives by day and by night to progress and advance along the path of human endeavor, whose most cherished desire is so to live and act as to enrich and illuminate the world, whose source of inspiration is the essence of Divine virtue, whose aim in life is so to conduct himself as to be the cause of infinite progress. Only when he attains unto such perfect gifts can it be said of him that he is a true Bahá'í. For in this holy Dispensation, the crowning glory of bygone ages, and cycles, true Faith is no mere acknowledgment of the Unity of God, but the living of a life that will manifest all the perfections and virtues implied in such belief. . . .   14

A PRAYER BY 'ABDU'L-BAHÁ

O Lord, I have turned my face unto Thy Kingdom of oneness and am immersed in the sea of Thy mercy! O Lord, enlighten my sight by beholding Thy lights in this dark night, and make me happy by the wine of Thy love in this wonderful age! O Lord, make me hear Thy call, and open before my face the doors of Thy heaven, so that I may see the light of Thy glory and become attracted to Thy beauty!

Verily, Thou art the Giver, the Generous, the Merciful, the Forgiving!

15

CHAPTER FOUR

PRAYER AND MEDITATION

BENEFITS OF PRAYER

AS TO thy question, "Why pray? What is the wisdom thereof, for God has established everything and executes all affairs after the best order and He ordains everything according to a becoming measure and puts things in their places with the greatest propriety and perfection—therefore what is the wisdom in beseeching and supplicating and in stating one's wants and seeking help?" Know thou, verily, it is becoming of a weak one to supplicate to the strong One and it behoveth a seeker of bounty to beseech the glorious, bountiful One. When one supplicates to his Lord, turns to Him and seeks bounty from His ocean this supplication is by itself a light to his heart, an illumination to his sight, a life to his soul and an exaltation to his being.

Therefore during thy supplications to God and thy reciting, "Thy name is my healing," consider how thy heart is cheered, thy soul delighted by the spirit of the love of God and thy mind attracted to the kingdom of God! By these attractions one's ability and capacity increase. When the vessel is widened the water increaseth and when the thirst grows the bounty of the cloud becomes agreeable to the taste of man. This is the mystery of supplication and the wisdom of stating one's wants.   1

O thou spiritual friend! Thou hast asked the wisdom of prayer. Know thou that prayer is indispensable and obligatory and man under no pretext whatsoever is excused therefrom unless he be mentally unsound or an insurmountable obstacle prevent him.

The wisdom of prayer is this, that it causes a connection between the servant and the True One, because in that state of prayer man with all his heart and soul turns his face towards His Highness the Almighty, seeking His association and desiring His love and compassion. The greatest happiness for a lover is to converse with his beloved, and the greatest gift for a seeker is to become familiar with the object of his longing. That is why the greatest hope of every soul who is attracted to the kingdom of God is to find an opportunity to entreat and supplicate at the ocean of His utterance, goodness and generosity.

Besides all this, prayer and fasting is the cause of awakening and mindfulness and is conducive to protection and preservation from tests. 2

Your faces shall be enlightened with the radiance of supplication to God (and) invocation to Him. 3

Know that in every home where God is praised and prayed to, and His kingdom proclaimed, that home is a garden of God and a paradise of His happiness. 4

. . . Whoso openeth his lips in this Day and maketh mention of the name of his Lord, the hosts of Divine inspiration shall descend upon him from the heaven of My name, the All-Knowing, the All-Wise. On him shall also descend the Concourse on high, each bearing aloft a chalice of pure light. Thus hath it been fore-ordained in the realm of God's revelation . . . 5

How to Pray

Know that nothing will benefit thee in this life save supplication and invocation unto God, service in His vineyard, and, with a heart full of love, to be in constant servitude unto Him. 6

Blessed is the man that hath, on the wings of longing, soared towards God, the Lord of the Judgment Day. 7

Set all thy hope in God and cleave tenaciously to His unfailing mercy. 8

O Son of Light! Forget all save Me and commune with My spirit. This is the essence of My command, therefore turn unto it. 9

Turn your faces away from the contemplation of your own finite selves and fix your eyes upon the Everlasting Radiance; then will your souls receive in full measure the Divine power of the Spirit and the blessings of the Infinite Bounty.   10

O Son of Spirit! Ask not of Me that which We desire not for thee, then be content with what We have ordained for thy sake, for this is that which profiteth thee, if therewith thou dost content thyself.   11

Commit thyself to God; give up thy will and choose that of God; abandon thy desire and lay hold on that of God.   12

The truest adorning (of the human heart) is the recognition of the truth that "He doeth whatsoever He willeth, and ordaineth that which He pleaseth."   13

Draw nigh unto God and persevere in (thy) communion with (or prayer to) thy Lord, so that the fire of God's love may glow more luminously in the heart, its heat grow stronger and give warmth to that region and its sound reach the Supreme Concourse.   14

O thou advancer toward the Kingdom! Endeavor thou day by day to increase thy yearning and attraction so that the attitude of supplication and prayer may be realized more often.   15

I render Thee thanks, O Thou Who hast lighted Thy fire within my soul, and cast the beams of light into my heart, that Thou hast taught Thy servants how to make mention of Thee, and revealed unto them the ways whereby they can supplicate Thee, through Thy most holy and exalted tongue, and Thy most august and precious speech. But for Thy leave, who is there that could venture to express Thy might and Thy grandeur; and were it not for Thine instruction, who is the man that could discover the ways of Thy pleasure in Thy creation?   16

A PRAYER OF 'ABDU'L-BAHÁ'S

In the Name of the Lord!

O Lord, my God and my Haven in my distress! My Shield and

my Shelter in my woes! My Asylum and Refuge in time of need and in my loneliness my Companion! In my anguish my Solace, and in my solitude a loving Friend. The Remover of the pangs of my sorrows and the Pardoner of my sins!

Wholly unto Thee do I turn, fervently imploring Thee with all my heart, my mind and my tongue, to shield me from all that runs counter to Thy will, in this, the Cycle of Thy Divine Unity, and to cleanse me of all defilement that will hinder me from seeking, stainless and unsullied, the shade of the tree of Thy grace.

Have mercy, O Lord, on the feeble, make whole the sick, and quench the burning thirst.

Gladden the bosom wherein the fire of Thy love doth smolder and set it aglow with the flame of Thy celestial love and spirit.

Robe the Tabernacles of Divine Unity with the vesture of holiness and set upon my head the crown of Thy favor.

Illumine my face with the radiance of the Orb of Thy bounty and graciously aid me in ministering at Thy holy threshold.

Make my heart overflow with love for Thy creatures and grant that I may become the sign of Thy mercy, the token of Thy grace, the promoter of concord amongst Thy loved ones, devoted unto Thee, uttering Thy commemoration, and forgetful of self but ever mindful of what is Thine.

O God! my God! Stay not from me the gentle gales of Thy pardon and grace and deprive me not of the wellsprings of Thine aid and favor.

'Neath the shade of Thy protecting wings let me nestle, and cast upon me the glance of Thine all-protecting eye.

Loose my tongue to laud Thy Name amidst Thy people, that my voice may be raised in great assemblies and from my lips may stream the flood of Thy praise.

Thou art, in all truth, the Gracious, the Glorified, the Mighty, the Omnipotent!   17

TWO PRAYERS OF THE BÁB

Is there any remover of difficulties save God! Say, Praise be to

God! He is God! All are His servants and all abide by His bidding!

Say: God sufficeth all things above all things, and nothing in the heavens or in the earth but God sufficeth. Verily, He is in Himself the Knower, the Sustainer, the Omnipotent.   18

WHAT TO PRAY FOR

Grief and sorrow do not come to us by chance, they are sent to us by the Divine Mercy for our own perfecting.

While a man is happy he may forget his God; but when grief comes and sorrows overwhelm him, then will he remember his Father Who is in Heaven, and Who is able to deliver him from his humiliations.   19

Endeavor and supplicate and pray God that, day unto day, thy firmness and steadfastness may grow and that thy countenance may radiate through the light of guidance.   20

Pray to God that He may strengthen you in divine virtue, so that you may be as angels in the world, and beacons of light to disclose the mysteries of the Kingdom to those with understanding hearts.   21

Forget all else save God, be in communion with Him, supplicate and pray to Him to make thee conqueror over the material things, impressed by the bounties of the Kingdom, commemorating the name of thy Lord, pure from all else save Him, and imbued with the spiritual attributes of those who are holy . . . then shall thy breaths have effect upon the hearts. . . .   22

Day and night I pray to Heaven for you that strength may be yours, and that, one and all, you may participate in the blessings of Bahá'u'lláh, and enter into the Kingdom.

I supplicate that you may become as new beings illumined with the Divine Light . . . and that from one end of Europe to the other the knowledge of the love of God may spread.

May this boundless love so fill your hearts and minds that sadness may find no room to enter.

May your eyes be opened to see the signs of the Kingdom of God, and may your ears be unstopped so that you may hear with a perfect understanding the heavenly Proclamation sounding in your midst.

May your souls receive help and comfort, and, being so strengthened, may they be enabled to live in accordance with the teachings of Bahá'u'lláh.

I pray for each and all that you may be as flames of love in the world, and that the brightness of your light and the warmth of your affection may reach the heart of every sad and sorrowing child of God.   23

Waft, then, unto me, O my God and my Beloved, from the right hand of Thy mercy and loving-kindness, the holy breaths of Thy favors, that they may draw me away from myself and from the world unto the courts of Thy nearness and Thy presence. Potent art Thou to do what pleaseth Thee. . . .   24

ANSWERS TO PRAYER

You have asked concerning approval of Christian Science treatment and healing. Spirit has influence; prayer has spiritual effect. Therefore we pray "O God! heal this sick one!" Perchance God will answer. Does it matter who prays? God will answer the prayer of every servant if that prayer is urgent. His mercy is vast, illimitable. He answers the prayers of all His servants. He answers the prayer of this plant. The plant prays potentially "O God! send me rain!" God answers the prayer and the plant grows. God will answer anyone. He answers prayers potentially. . . .

. . . Did we not pray potentially for needed blessings before we were created? When we came into this world did we not find our prayers answered? Did we not find mother, father, food, light, home and every other necessity and blessing, although we did not actually ask for them? Therefore it is natural that God will give to us when we ask Him. His mercy is all-encircling.

But we ask for things which the divine wisdom does not desire for us and there is no answer to our prayer. . . . We pray, "O

God! make me wealthy!" If this prayer were universally answered, human affairs would be at a standstill. There would be none left to work in the streets, none to till the soil, none to build, none to run the trains. . . . The affairs of the world would be interfered with, energies crippled and progress hindered. But whatever we ask for, which is in accord with divine wisdom, God will answer.

For instance, a very feeble patient may ask the doctor to give him food which would be positively dangerous to his life and condition. He may beg for roast meat. The doctor is kind and wise. He knows it would be dangerous to his patient so he refuses to allow it. The doctor is merciful; the patient ignorant. Through the doctor's kindness the patient recovers; his life is saved. Yet the patient may cry out that the doctor is unkind, not good, because he refuses to answer his pleading.

God is merciful. In His mercy He answers the prayers of all His servants when according to His supreme wisdom it is necessary.   25

A servant is drawn unto Me through prayers until I answer Him; and when I have answered his prayers, I become the ear wherewith he heareth.   26

I give praise unto Thee, O my God, that Thou hast awakened me out of my sleep, and brought me forth after my disappearance and raised me up from my slumber. I have wakened this morning with my face set toward the splendors of the Day-Star of Thy Revelation, through which the Heavens of Thy power and Thy majesty have been illumined, acknowledging Thy signs, believing in Thy Book, and holding fast unto Thy cord. . . .

Do Thou ordain for me, O my Lord, the good of this world and of the next. I testify that within Thy grasp are held the reins of all things. Thou changest them as Thou pleasest. No God is there save Thee, the Strong, the Faithful.

Thou art He Who changeth through His bidding abasement into glory, and weakness into strength, and powerlessness into might, and fear into calm, and doubt into certainty. No God is there but Thee, the Mighty, the Beneficent.

Thou disappointest no one who hath sought Thee, nor dost Thou keep back from Thee any one who hath desired Thee. Ordain Thou for me what becometh the heaven of Thy generosity, and the ocean of Thy bounty. Thou art, verily, the Almighty, the Most Powerful. 27

Therefore strive that your actions day by day may be beautiful prayers. Turn towards God, and seek always to do that which is right and noble. · 28

WHEN TO PRAY

Supplicate to God, pray to Him and invoke Him at midnight and at dawn. Be humble and submissive to God and chant the verses of thanksgiving at morn and eve . . . 29

At the dawn of every day he (the true seeker) should commune with God, and with all his soul persevere in the quest of his Beloved. 30

Supplication to God at morn and eve is conducive to the joy of hearts and prayer causes spirituality and fragrance. Thou shouldst necessarily continue therein. 31

Trust in the favors of Thy Lord; supplicate unto Him and beseech in the middle of the night and at early morn just as a needy and captive one beseeches. It is incumbent upon thee to turn unto the Kingdom of God and to pray, supplicate and invoke during all times. This is the means by which thy soul shall ascend upward to the apex of the gift of God. 32

PRAYER FOR OTHERS

In these (warring) countries there is hardly a house free from the sound of bitter weeping, scarcely can one find a home untouched by the cruel hand of war.

Alas! we see on all sides how cruel, prejudiced and unjust is man, and how slow he is to believe in God and follow His commandments.

Why is man so hard of heart? It is because he does not yet know God. If he had knowledge of God he could not act in direct opposition to His laws. If only the laws and precepts of the Prophets of God had been believed, understood and followed, wars would no longer darken the face of the earth.

If man had even the rudiments of justice, such a state of things would be impossible.

Therefore, I say unto you pray—pray and turn your faces to God, that He, in His infinite compassion and mercy, may help and succor these misguided ones. Pray that He will grant them spiritual understanding and teach them tolerance and mercy, that the eyes of their minds may be opened and that they may be endued with the gift of the Spirit. . . . I beseech you all to pray with heart and soul that this may be accomplished. 33

With all his heart should the seeker avoid fellowship with evil doers, and pray for the remission of their sins. 34

Pray thou that the ill-natured become good-natured and the weak become strong. 35

Reflect awhile and consider how they that are the loved ones of God must conduct themselves, and to what heights they must soar. Beseech thou, at all times, Thy Lord, the God of Mercy, to aid them to do what He willeth. He, verily is the Most Powerful, the All-Glorious. 36

O maid-servant of God! Do beseech and pray constantly for 'Abdu'l-Bahá and beg the confirmation and assistance of God in his behalf, because I am earnestly fond of the prayers of the maid-servants of God in my behalf, and of their asking the blessing of God for this servant.

I begged of God to ordain all good for thee for thy praying for 'Abdu'l-Bahá. 37

. . . Establish a spiritual meeting-place wherefrom the incense of sanctity and purity will rise up to God, assemble there with fragrance and spirituality and celebrate the Name of your Lord by day and by night. 38

Supplication and prayer on behalf of others will surely be effective. When hearts are united, when faces are turned towards the Kingdom of Abhá, surely enlightenment will be the result.

39

As the spirit of man after putting off this material form has an everlasting life, certainly any existing being is capable of making progress; therefore it is permitted to ask for advancement, forgiveness, mercy, beneficence, and blessings for a man after his death, because existence is capable of progression. That is why in the prayers of Bahá'u'lláh, forgiveness and remission of sins are asked for those who have died. Moreover, as people in this world are in need of God, they will also need Him in the other world. The creatures are always in need, and God is absolutely independent, whether in this world or in the world to come.

The wealth of the other world is nearness to God. Consequently it is certain that those who are near the Divine Court are allowed to intercede, and this intercession is approved by God. But intercession in the other world is not like intercession in this world: it is another thing, another reality, which cannot be expressed in words.

40

GRATITUDE AND PRAISE

Do you realize how much you should thank God for His blessings? If you should thank Him a thousand times with each breath it would not be sufficient, because God has created and trained you. He has protected you from every affliction and prepared every gift and bestowal. Consider what a kind Father He is. . . . He has given us a kind father and compassionate mother, . . . refreshing water, gentle breezes and the sun shining above our heads. In brief, He has supplied all the necessities of life although we did not ask for any of these great gifts. . . . He has created us in this radiant century, a century longed for and expected by all the sanctified souls in past periods. . . . The philosophers of history have agreed that this century is equal to one hundred past centuries. This is true from every standpoint.

This is the century of science, inventions, discoveries and universal laws. This is the century of the revelation of the mysteries of God. . . . Therefore you must render thanks and glorification to God that you were born in this age. Furthermore you have listened to the call of Bahá'u'lláh. . . . You were asleep; you are awakened. Your ears are attentive; your hearts are informed. You have acquired the love of God. You have attained to the knowledge of God. This is the most great bestowal of God. . . . You must appreciate the value of this bounty and engage your time in mentioning and thanking the True One. You must live in the utmost happiness. If any trouble or vicissitude comes into your lives, if your heart is depressed on account of health, livelihood or vocation, let not these things affect you. They should not cause unhappiness, for Bahá'u'lláh has brought you divine happiness. . . . Render continual thanks unto God so that the confirmations of God may encircle you all.   41

Be thou happy and well pleased and arise to offer thanks to God, in order that thanksgiving may conduce to the increase of bounty.   42

Thank thou the kind Father . . . that the world of creation and the heart of the universe found comfort in His mercy.   43

Reflect upon this: What a bounty and what a favor it is that the sages of the world and the wise among mankind are incompetent of comprehension, yet the little children of the Kingdom have attained the Truth, dwell and abide under the shadow of the Tree of Life and are assisted by the eternal and everlasting gift!   44

Wherefore be thankful to God, for having strengthened thee to aid His Cause, for having made the flowers of knowledge and understanding to spring forth in the garden of thine heart. Thus hath His grace encompassed thee, and encompassed the whole of creation. Beware, lest thou allow anything whatsoever to grieve thee.   45

O Son of Being! Make mention of Me on My earth, that in My

heaven I may remember thee, thus shall Mine eyes and thine be solaced. 46

I give praise to Thee, O my God, that the fragrance of Thy loving-kindness hath enraptured me, and the gentle winds of Thy mercy have inclined me in the direction of Thy bountiful favors. 47

Glory be to Thee, O my God! The power of Thy might beareth me witness! I can have no doubt that should the holy breaths of Thy loving-kindness and the breeze of Thy bountiful favor cease, for less than the twinkling of an eye, to breathe over all created things, the entire creation would perish, and all that are in heaven and earth would be reduced to utter nothingness. Magnified, therefore, be the marvellous evidences of Thy transcendent power! Magnified be the potency of Thine exalted might! Magnified be the majesty of Thine all-encompassing greatness, and the energizing influence of Thy will! 48

Exalted art Thou above my praise and the praise of any one beside me, above my description and the description of all who are in heaven and all who are on earth! 49

Magnified be Thy name, O my God, for that Thou hast manifested the Day which is the King of Days, the Day which Thou didst announce unto Thy chosen ones and Thy Prophets in Thy most excellent Tablets, the Day whereon Thou didst shed the splendor of the glory of all Thy names upon all created things. 50

Intone, O My servant, the verses of God that have been received by thee, as intoned by them that have drawn nigh unto Him, that the sweetness of Thy melody may kindle thine own soul, and attract the hearts of all men. Whoso reciteth, in the privacy of his chamber, the verses revealed by God, the scattering angels of the Almighty shall scatter abroad the fragrance of the words uttered by his mouth, and shall cause the heart of every righteous man to throb. Though he may, at first, remain unaware of its effect, yet the virtue of the grace vouchsafed unto him must needs sooner or later exercise its influence upon his soul. 51

THE GRATITUDE OF BAHÁ'U'LLÁH

Glorified art Thou, O my God! Thou knowest that my sole aim in revealing Thy Cause hath been to reveal Thee and not myself, and to manifest Thy glory rather than my glory. In Thy path and to attain Thy pleasure, I have scorned rest, joy, delight. At all times and under all conditions my gaze hath been fixed on Thy precepts, and mine eyes bent upon the things Thou hast bidden me observe in Thy Tablets. I have wakened every morning to the light of Thy praise and Thy remembrance, and reached every evening inhaling the fragrance of Thy mercy.   52

Every time I lift mine eyes unto Thy heaven, I call to mind Thy highness and Thy loftiness, and Thine incomparable glory and greatness; and every time I turn my gaze to Thine earth, I am made to recognize the evidences of Thy power and the tokens of Thy bounty. And when I behold the sea, I find that it speaketh to me of Thy majesty, and of the potency of Thy might, and of Thy sovereignty and of Thy grandeur. And at whatever time I contemplate the mountains, I am led to discover the ensigns of Thy victory and the standards of Thine omnipotence.   53

Every trouble that hath touched me in Thy path hath added to my joy and increased my gladness. I swear by Thee, O Thou Who art the King of Kings! None of the kings of the earth hath power to hinder me from remembering Thee or from extolling Thy virtues.   54

I yield Thee such thanks, as can direct the steps of the wayward towards the splendors of the morning light of Thy guidance. . . . I yield Thee such thanks as can cause the sick to draw nigh unto the waters of Thy healing, and can help those who are far from Thee to approach the living fountain of Thy presence. . . . I yield Thee such thanks as can stir up all things to extol Thee . . . and can unloose the tongues of all beings to . . . magnify Thy beauty . . . I yield Thee such thanks as can make the corrupt tree to bring forth good fruit . . . and revive the bodies of all beings with the gentle winds of Thy transcendent grace . . . I yield Thee such thanks as can cause Thee to forgive all sins and trespasses, and to fulfill the needs of the peoples of all religions, and to waft the fragrances of pardon over the entire creation . . . I yield Thee such thanks as can satisfy the wants of all such as seek Thee, and realize the aims of them that have recognized Thee. I yield Thee such thanks as can blot out from the hearts of men all suggestions of limitations . . .   55

Meditation and the Revealed Word of God

One hour's reflection is preferable to seventy years of pious worship.   56

Through the faculty of meditation man attains to eternal life; Through it he receives the breath of the Holy Spirit—the bestowal of the Spirit is given in reflection and meditation.

This faculty of meditation frees man from the animal nature, discerns the reality of things, puts man in touch with God.

This faculty brings forth from the invisible plane the sciences and arts. Through the meditative faculty inventions are made possible, colossal undertakings are carried out; through it governments can run smoothly. Through this faculty man enters into the very Kingdom of God. . . .

Nevertheless some thoughts are useless to man; they are like waves moving in the sea without result. But if the faculty of meditation is bathed in the inner light and characterized with divine attributes, the results will be confirmed.

The meditative faculty is akin to the mirror; if you put it before earthly objects it will reflect them. Therefore if the spirit of man is contemplating earthly subjects he will be informed of these.

But if you turn the mirror of your spirits heavenwards . . . the rays of the Sun of Reality will be reflected in your hearts, and the virtues of the Kingdom will be obtained.

Therefore let us keep this faculty rightly directed—turning it to the heavenly Sun and not to earthly objects—so that we may discover the secrets of the Kingdom, and comprehend the allegories of the Bible and the mysteries of the Spirit.   57

Investigate and study the Holy Scriptures word by word so that you may attain knowledge of the mysteries hidden therein. Be not satisfied with words, but seek to understand the spiritual meanings hidden in the heart of the words. . . .

For instance, . . . consider the symbolical meanings of the words and teachings of Christ. His Holiness said, "I am the living bread which came down from heaven; if any man eat of this bread he shall live forever." When the Jews heard this they took it literally and failed to understand the significance of His meaning and teaching. The spiritual truth which Christ wished to convey to them was that the reality of Divinity within Him was like a blessing which had come down from heaven and that he who partook of this blessing should never die. That is to say, "bread" was the symbol of the perfections which had descended upon Him from God, and he who ate of this bread or endowed himself with the perfections of Christ would undoubtedly attain to life everlasting. The Jews did not understand Him, and taking the words literally said, "How can this man give us his flesh to eat?" Had they understood the real meaning of the Holy Book they would have become believers in Christ.

All the texts and teachings of the Holy Testaments have intrinsic spiritual meanings. They are not to be taken literally. . . . These are the mysteries of God. . . . I therefore pray in your behalf that you may be given the power of understanding these inner real meanings of the Holy Scriptures and may become informed of the mysteries deposited in the words of the Bible so that you may attain eternal life and that your hearts may be attracted to the Kingdom of God. May your souls be illumined by the light of the words of God and may you become repositories of the mysteries of God, for no comfort is greater and no happiness is sweeter than spiritual comprehension of the Divine teachings. 58

Chant (or recite) the words of God every morning and evening. The one who neglects this has not been faithful to the Covenant of God and His agreement, and he who turns away from it today is of those who have turned away from God.

Fear God, O my people! Let not too much reading (of the Sacred Word) . . . make you proud. To chant but one verse with joy and gladness is better for you than reading all the revelations of the omnipotent God with carelessness. Chant the Tablets of God in such measure that ye be not overtaken with fatigue and depression. Burden not the soul so as to cause exhaustion and languor, but rather refresh it that thus it may soar on the wings of revelation to the Dawning-place of proofs. This brings you nearer to God, were ye of those who understand.   59

Immerse yourselves in the ocean of My words, that ye may unravel its secrets, and discover all the pearls of wisdom that lie hid in its depths.   60

Chapter Five

THE POWER OF THE HOLY SPIRIT

What Is the Holy Spirit?

THE Holy Spirit is the Mediator between God and His creatures. It is like a mirror facing the sun. As the pure mirror receives light from the sun and transmits this bounty to others, so the Holy Spirit is the mediator of the Holy Light from the Sun of Reality, which it gives to the sanctified realities. It is adorned with all the divine perfections. Every time it appears the world is renewed, and a new cycle is founded. The body of the world of humanity puts on a new garment. It can be compared to the spring; whenever it comes the world passes from one condition to another. Through the advent of spring the earth becomes verdant and blooming, and all sorts of flowers and sweet-scented herbs grow; the trees have new life, new fruits appear, and a new cycle is founded. The appearance of the Holy Spirit is like this. Whenever it appears, it renews the world of humanity and gives a new spirit to the human realities; it arrays the world of existence in a praiseworthy garment, dispels the darkness of ignorance and causes the radiation of the light of perfections. Christ with this power has renewed this cycle; the heavenly spring with the utmost freshness and sweetness spread its tent in the world of humanity and the life-giving breeze perfumed the nostrils of the enlightened ones.

In the same way, the appearance of Bahá'u'lláh was like a new springtime which appeared with holy breezes, with the hosts of everlasting life, and with heavenly power. It established the Throne of the Divine Kingdom in the center of the world, and by

the power of the Holy Spirit revived souls and established a
new cycle.   1

The Divine Reality is Unthinkable, Limitless, Eternal, Immortal and Invisible.

The world of creation is bound by natural law, finite and
mortal.

The Infinite Reality cannot be said to ascend or descend. It is
beyond the understanding of man, and cannot be described in
terms which apply to the phenomenal sphere of the created
world.

Man, then, is in extreme need of the only Power by which he is
able to receive help from the Divine Reality, that Power alone
bringing him into contact with the Source of all life.

An intermediary is needed to bring two extremes into relation
with each other. Riches and poverty, plenty and need; without
an intermediary power there could be no relation between these
pairs of opposites.

So we can say that there must be a Mediator between God and
man, and this is none other than the Holy Spirit, which brings
the created earth into relation with the "Unthinkable One," the
Divine Reality.

The Divine Reality may be likened to the sun and the Holy
Spirit to the rays of the sun. As the rays of the sun bring the
light and warmth of the sun to the earth, giving life to all created
beings, so do the "Manifestations" bring the power of the Holy
Spirit from the Divine Sun of Reality to give Light and Life to
the souls of men. . . .

The Holy Spirit it is, which, through the mediation of the
Prophets of God, teaches spiritual virtues to man and enables him
to attain Eternal life.   2

It is evident that the souls receive grace from the bounty of
the Holy Spirit which appears in the Manifestations of God, and
not from the personality of the Manifestation.   3

. . . The spirit of man is not illumined and quickened
through material sources. It is not resuscitated by investigating
phenomena of the world of matter. The spirit of man is in need

of the protection of the Holy Spirit. Just as he advances by progressive stages from the mere physical world of being into the intellectual realm, so must he develop upward in moral attributes and spiritual graces. In the process of this attainment he is ever in need of the bestowals of the Holy Spirit. Material development may be likened to the glass of a lamp whereas divine virtues and spiritual susceptibilities are the light within the glass. The lamp chimney is worthless without the light; likewise man in his material condition requires the radiance and vivification of the divine virtues and merciful attributes. Without the presence of the Holy Spirit he is lifeless. Although physically and mentally alive he is spiritually dead. His Holiness Christ announced, "That which is born of flesh is flesh and that which is born of spirit is spirit," meaning that man must be born again. As the babe is born into the light of this physical world so must the physical and intellectual man be born into the light of the world of divinity.   4

ITS POWER

When Christ apeared with those marvelous breaths of the Holy Spirit, the children of Israel said, "We are quite independent of Him; we can do without Him and follow Moses; we have a book and in it are found the teachings of God; what need therefore have we of this man?" Christ said to them, "The book sufficeth you not." It is possible for a man to hold to a book of medicine and say, "I have no need of a doctor; I will act according to the book; in it every disease is named, all symptoms are explained, the diagnosis of each ailment is completely written out and a prescription for each malady is furnished; therefore why do I need a doctor?" This is sheer ignorance. A physician is needed to prescribe. Through his skill, the principles of the book are correctly and effectively applied until the patient is restored to health. Christ was a heavenly physician. He brought spiritual health and healing into the world. Bahá'u'lláh is likewise a divine physician. He has revealed prescriptions for removing disease from the body-politic and has remedied human conditions by spiritual power.   5

To gain control over physical bodies is an extremely easy matter, but to bring spirits within the bonds of serenity is a most arduous undertaking. This is not the work of everybody. It necessitates a Divine and holy potency, the potency of inspiration, the power of the Holy Spirit. For example, His Holiness Christ was capable of leading spirits into that abode of serenity. He was capable of guiding hearts into that haven of rest. From the day of His manifestation to the present time He has been resuscitating hearts and quickening spirits. He has exercised that vivifying influence in the realm of hearts and spirits; therefore His resuscitating is everlasting. In this century of the "latter times" Bahá'u'lláh has appeared and so resuscitated spirits that they have manifested powers more than human. Thousands of His followers have given their lives and while under sword, shedding their blood, they have proclaimed "Yá-Bahá'u'l-Abhá!"* Such resuscitation is impossible except through a heavenly potency, a power supernatural, the Divine power of the Holy Spirit.

6

We understand that the Holy Spirit is the energizing factor in the life of man. Whosoever receives this power is able to influence all with whom he comes in contact. . . .

The difference between spiritual philosophers and others is shown by their lives. The Spiritual Teacher shows his belief in his own teaching by himself *being* what he recommends to others.

An humble man without learning, but filled with the Holy Spirit, is more powerful than the most profound scholar, without that inspiration. He who is educated by the Divine Spirit can, in his time, lead others to receive the same Spirit.

I pray for you that you may be informed by the life of the Divine Spirit, so that you may be the means of educating others. The life and morals of a spiritual man are, in themselves, an education to those who know him.

Think not of your own limitations, dwell only on the welfare

---

* O Thou Glory of the Most Glorious!

of the Kingdom of Glory. Consider the influence of Jesus Christ on His Apostles, then think of their effect upon the world.

These simple men were enabled by the Power of the Holy Spirit to spread the glad tidings!

So may you all receive Divine assistance! No capacity is limited when led by the Spirit of God!   7

How to Attract the Power of the Holy Spirit

Know thou that the Messianic Spirit and the outpouring of the Holy Spirit is always manifest, but capacity and ability (to receive it) is more in some and less in others. After the Crucifixion the Apostles had not in the beginning the capacity and ability to witness the Messianic reality; for they were agitated. But when they found firmness and steadfastness, their inner sight became opened, and they saw the reality of the Messiah as manifest.   8

A soul who is firm will become a son of the Kingdom of God and will be confirmed with the power of the Holy Spirit.   9

The Holy Spirit speaketh to the pure hearts and to the good and righteous souls in every spot of the earth. . . . Turn thyself wholly to it—thus thou shalt be enabled to ascertain its influence and power, the strength of its life and the greatness of its confirmation.   10

Do not look at your weakness, nay, rely upon the confirmation of the Holy Spirit. Verily, it maketh the weak strong, the lowly mighty, the child grown. . . and the small great.   11

The Holy Spirit breathes in this day unto the hearts which are moving, beating, pure and attracted by the love of God.   12

I now assure thee, O servant of God, that, if thy mind become empty and pure from every mention and thought and thy heart attracted wholly to the Kingdom of God, forgetting all else besides God and coming into communion with the Spirit of God, then the Holy Spirit will assist thee with a power which will enable thee to penetrate all things, and a Dazzling Spark which enlightens all sides; a Brilliant Flame in the zenith of the heavens, will teach thee that which thou dost not know of the facts of the universe and of the divine doctrine. Verily, I say unto thee, every soul that ariseth today to guide others to the path of safety and infuse into them the Spirit of Life, the Holy Spirit will inspire that soul with evidences, proofs and facts, and the lights will shine upon it from the Kingdom of God. Do not forget what I have conveyed unto thee from the breath of the Spirit. Verily it is the shining morn and the rosy dawn which will impart unto thee the lights, reveal the mysteries and make thee competent in science, and through it the pictures of the Supreme World will be printed in thy heart and the facts of the secrets of the Kingdom of God will shine before thee.   13

Chapter Six

FAITH AND CERTITUDE

Faith an Awareness of the Sovereignty of God

THE Hand of Omnipotence hath established His Revelation upon an unassailable, an enduring foundation. Storms of human strife are powerless to undermine its basis, nor will men's fanciful theories succeed in damaging its structure.　　　1

I testify, O my God, to that whereunto Thy chosen Ones have testified and acknowledge that which the inmates of the all-highest Paradise and those who have circled round Thy mighty Throne have acknowledged. The kingdoms of earth and heaven are Thine, O Lord of the worlds!　　　2

Signs of True Faith

Although a person of good deeds is acceptable at the threshold of the Almighty, yet it is first "to know" and then "to do." Although a blind man produceth a most wonderful and exquisite art, yet he is deprived of seeing it. Consider how most animals labor for man, draw loads and facilitate travel; yet, as they are ignorant, they receive no reward for this toil and labor. The cloud raineth, roses and hyacinths grow; the plain and meadow, the garden and trees become green and blossom; yet they do not realize the results and outcome of all these. The lamp is lighted, but as it hath not a conscious knowledge of itself, no one hath become glad because of it. Moreover, a soul of excellent deeds and good manners will undoubtedly advance, from whatever horizon he beholdeth the lights radiating. Herein lies the difference: By faith is meant, first, conscious knowledge, and second, the practice of good deeds.　　　3

Blessed is the man that hath acknowledged his belief in God and in His signs, and recognized that "He shall not be asked of His doings." Such a recognition hath been made by God the ornament of every belief, and its very foundation. Upon it must depend the acceptance of every goodly deed. Fasten your eyes upon it, that haply the whisperings of the rebellious may not cause you to slip. . . . He that hath acknowledged this principle will be endowed with the most perfect constancy. Such is the teaching which God bestoweth upon you, a teaching which will deliver you from all manner of doubt and perplexity, and enable you to attain unto salvation in both this world and the next. He, verily, is the Ever-Forgiving, the Most Bountiful. 4

Now faith is assurance of things hoped for, a conviction of things not seen. . . . By faith we understand that the worlds have been framed by the Word of God, so that what is seen hath not been made out of things which appear. . . .

He that cometh to God must believe that He is, and that He is a rewarder of them that seek after Him. By faith Noah, being warned of God of things not seen as yet, moved with godly fear, prepared an ark to the saving of his house. . . . By faith Abraham, when he was called, obeyed to go out unto a place which he was to receive for an inheritance; and he went out, not knowing whither he went. By faith he became a sojourner in the land of promise, as in a land not his own, dwelling in tents, with Isaac and Jacob, the heirs with him of the same promise. For he looked for the city which hath foundations, whose builder and maker is God. By faith Moses forsook Egypt, not fearing the wrath of the king, for he endured as seeing Him who is invisible. . . .

And what more shall I say? for the time will fail me if I tell of Gideon, . . . of David and Samuel and the prophets, who through faith subdued kingdoms, wrought righteousness, obtained promises, stopped the mouths of lions, quenched the power of fire, escaped the edge of the sword, from weakness were made strong. . . . Others had trials of mockings and scourgings, yea, moreover of bonds and imprisonment; they were stoned, they were sawn asunder, they were tempted, they were slain with the

sword: they went about in sheepskins, in goatskins, being destitute, afflicted, ill-treated—of whom the world was not worthy—
wandering in deserts and mountains and caves and the holes of
the earth. . . .

Therefore, let us also, seeing we are compassed about with so
great a cloud of witnesses, lay aside every weight and the sin
which doth so easily beset us, and let us run with patience the
race that is set before us.   5

In this most resplendent Dispensation, this most mighty Sovereignty, a number of illumined divines, of men of consummate
learning, of doctors of mature wisdom, have attained unto His
Court, drunk the cup of His divine Presence, and been invested
with the honor of His most excellent favor. They have renounced for the sake of the Beloved, the world and all that is
therein. . . .

All these were guided by the light of that Sun of divine Revelation, confessed and acknowledged His truth. Such was their
faith that most of them renounced their substance and kindred,
and cleaved to the good-pleasure of the All-Glorious. They laid
down their lives for their Well-Beloved, and surrendered their
all in His path. Their breasts were made targets for the darts of
the enemy, and their heads adorned the spears of the infidel. No
land remained which did not drink the blood of these embodi-
ments of detachment, and no sword that did not bruise their
necks. Their deeds alone testify to the truth of their words.   6

The essence of faith is fewness of words and abundance of
deeds; he whose words exceed his deeds, know verily his death is
better than his life. . . .   7

Just as the conception of faith hath existed from the beginning
that hath no beginning, and will endure to the end that hath no
end, in like manner will the true believer eternally live and endure. His spirit will everlastingly circle round the Will of God.
He will last as long as God Himself will last. . . . It is evident
that the loftiest mansions in the Realm of Immortality have been
ordained as the habitation of them that have truly believed in
God and in His signs. Death can never invade that holy seat.   8

He that partaketh of the waters of My Revelation will taste all the incorruptible delights ordained by God from the beginning that hath no beginning to the end that hath no end.   9

The first sign of faith is Love.   10

Verily I read thy letter, which indicated that the Truth (of God) hath revealed itself unto thee, that thy fear is quieted and that thou hast attained unto composure, assuredly believing in this great Cause.

Know thou, verily, there are many veils in which the Truth is enveloped; gloomy veils; then delicate and transparent veils; then the envelopment of Light, the sight of which dazzles the eyes. . . .   11

Faith is the magnet which draws the confirmation of the Merciful One. Service is the magnet which attracts the heavenly strength. I hope thou wilt attain both.   12

How Is FAITH GAINED?

Rely upon God, thy God and the Lord of thy fathers. For the people are wandering in the paths of delusion, bereft of discernment to see God with their own eyes, or hear His Melody with their own ears.   13

. . . Every man hath been, and will continue to be, able of himself to appreciate the Beauty of God, the Glorified. Had he not been endowed with such a capacity, how could he be called to account for his failure? If, in the day when all the peoples of the earth will be gathered together, any man should reply and say: "Inasmuch as all men have erred, and none hath been found willing to turn his face to the Truth, I, too, following their example, have grievously failed to recognize the Beauty of the Eternal," such a plea will, assuredly, be rejected. For the faith of no man can be conditioned by any one except himself.   14

If thou wishest the divine knowledge and recognition, purify thy heart from all beside God, be wholly attracted to the ideal, beloved One; search for and choose Him and apply thyself to rational and authoritative arguments. For arguments are a guide to the path and by this the heart will be turned unto the Sun of Truth. And when the heart is turned unto the Sun, then the eye will be opened and will recognize the Sun through the Sun itself. Then (man) will be in no need of arguments (or proofs), for the sun is altogether independent, and absolute independence is in need of nothing, and proofs are one of the things (of which absolute independence has no need). Be not like Thomas; be thou like Peter.   15

Only when the lamp of search, of earnest striving, of longing desire, of passionate devotion, of fervid love, of rapture, and ecstasy, is kindled within the seeker's heart, and the breeze of His loving-kindness is wafted upon his soul, will the darkness of error be dispelled, the mists of doubts and misgivings be dissipated, and the lights of knowledge and certitude envelop his being.   16

Verily, I beseech the Lord of Hosts to increase thy faith each day over that of the previous day.   17

Be confident in the bounty of thy Lord.   18

Say: The first and foremost testimony establishing His truth is His own Self. Next to this testimony is His Revelation. For whoso faileth to recognize either the one or the other He hath established the words He hath revealed as proof of His reality and truth. This is, verily, an evidence of His tender mercy unto men. He hath endowed every soul with the capacity to recognize the signs of God. . . . He will never deal unjustly with any one, neither will he task a soul beyond its power. He, verily, is the Compassionate, the All-Merciful.   19

Faith in God, and the knowledge of Him, cannot be fully realized except through believing in all that hath proceeded from Him (the Manifestation), and by practicing all that He hath commanded and all that is revealed in the Book from the Supreme Pen.   20

CHAPTER SEVEN

HEALING AND HEALTH

DIFFERENT KINDS OF HEALING

THERE are two ways of healing sickness, material means and spiritual means. The first is by the use of remedies, of medicines; the second consists in praying to God and in turning to Him. Both means should be used and practiced.

Illness caused by physical accident should be treated with medical remedies; those which are due to spiritual causes disappear through spiritual means. Thus an illness caused by affliction, fear, nervous impressions, will be healed by spiritual rather than by physical treatment. Hence, both kinds of remedies should be considered. Moreover they are not contradictory, and thou shouldst accept the physical remedies as coming from the mercy and favor of God, Who hath revealed and made manifest medical science so that His servants may profit from this kind of treatment also. Thou shouldst give equal attention to spiritual treatments, for they produce marvelous effects.

Now, if thou wishest to know the Divine remedy which will heal man from all sickness and will give him the health of the Divine Kingdom, know that it is the precepts and teachings of God. Guard them sacredly.   1

Should ye be attacked by illness or disease, consult skillful physicians. . . .

Do not neglect medical treatment when it is necessary, but leave it off when health has been restored. Treat disease through diet, by preference, refraining from the use of drugs; and if you find what is required in a single herb, do not resort to a com-

pounded medicament. . . . Abstain from drugs when the health
is good, but administer them when necessary.   2

When . . . the science of medicine . . . has reached maturity cures will be performed by things which are not repulsive
to the smell and taste of man; that is to say by aliments, fruits
and vegetables which are agreeable to the taste and have an agreeable smell. . .
The cause of the entrance of disease into the human body is
either a physical one or is the effect of excitement of the nerves.
But the principal causes of disease are physical; for the human
body is composed of numerous elements, but in the measure of
an especial equilibrium. As long as this equilibrium is main-
tained, man is preserved from disease; but if this essential balance,
which is the pivot of the constitution is disturbed, the constitution is disordered, and disease will supervene.
. . . So long as the aim is the readjustment of the constituents
of the body, it can be effected either by medicine or by food.
. . .
It is therefore evident that it is possible to cure by foods, aliments and fruits; but as today the science of medicine is imperfect, this fact is not yet fully grasped. When the science of
medicine reaches perfection, treatment will be given by foods, aliments, fragrant fruits, and vegetables, and by various waters,
hot and cold in temperature.   3

(Healing may result) from the entire concentration of the
mind of a strong person upon a sick person, when the latter expects with all his concentrated faith that a cure will be effected
from the spiritual power of the strong person to such an extent
that there will be a cordial connection between the strong person
and the invalid. The strong person makes every effort to cure the
sick patient, and the sick patient is then sure of receiving a cure.
From the effect of these mental impressions an excitement of the
nerves is produced, and this impression and this excitement of the
nerves will become the cause of the recovery of the sick person.
So when a sick person has a strong desire and intense hope for
something, and hears suddenly the tidings of its realization, a

nervous excitement is produced, which will make the malady entirely disappear. In the same way, if a cause of terror suddenly occurs, perhaps an excitement may be produced in the nerves of a strong (well) person, which will immediately cause a malady. The cause of the sickness will be no material thing, for that person has not eaten anything, and nothing harmful has touched him; the excitement of the nerves is then the only cause of the illness. In the same way the sudden realization of a chief desire will give such joy that the nerves will be excited by it, and this excitement may produce health.

To conclude, the complete and perfect connection between the spiritual doctor and the sick person—that is, a connection of such a kind that the spiritual doctor entirely concentrates himself, and all the attention of the sick person is given to the spiritual doctor from whom he expects to realize health—causes an excitement of the nerves, and health is produced.

But all this has effect only to a certain extent, and that not always. For if some one is afflicted with a very violent disease, or is wounded, these means will not remove the disease nor close and heal the wound. That is to say, these means have no power in severe maladies, unless the constitution helps, because a strong constitution often overcomes disease.

But (another) kind of healing is produced through the power of the Holy Spirit. This does not depend on contact, nor on sight, nor upon presence; it is not dependent upon any condition. Whether the disease be light or severe, whether there be a contact of bodies or not, whether a personal connection be established between the sick person and the healer or not, this healing takes place through the power of the Holy Spirit.   4

Joy gives us wings! In times of joy our strength is more vital, our intellect keener. . . . But when sadness visits us our strength leaves us.   5

All true healing comes from God. There are two causes for sickness, one is material, the other spiritual. If the sickness is of the body, a material remedy is needed, if of the soul, a spiritual remedy.

If the heavenly benediction be upon us while we are being healed then only can we be made whole, for medicine is but the outward and visible means through which we can obtain the heavenly healing. Unless the spirit be healed, the cure of the body is worth nothing. All is in the hands of God, and without Him there can be no health in us.   6

HEALING AS AN ANSWER TO PRAYER

Without the help of God man is even as the beasts that perish, but God has bestowed such wonderful power upon him that he might ever look upward, and receive, among other gifts, healing from His Divine Bounty.   7

O thou pure and spiritual one!
Turn thou toward God with thy heart beating with His love, devoted to His praise, gazing toward His Kingdom and seeking help from His Holy Spirit in a state of ecstasy, rapture, love, yearning, joy and fragrance. God will assist thee, through a Spirit from His Presence, to heal sickness and diseases.   8

You have asked concerning approval of Christian Science treatment and healing. Spirit has influence; prayer has spiritual effect. Therefore we pray, "O God! heal this sick one!" Perchance God will answer. Does it matter who prays? God will answer the prayer of every servant if that prayer is urgent. His mercy is vast, illimitable.   9

In God must be our trust. There is no God but Him, the Healer, the Knower, the Helper. . . . Nothing in earth or heaven is outside the grasp of God.
O physician! In treating the sick, first mention the name of Thy God, the Possessor of the Day of Judgment and then use what God hath destined for the healing of His creatures. By My Life! The physician who has drunk from the Wine of My Love, his visit is healing, and his breath is mercy and hope. Cling to him for the welfare of the constitution. He is confirmed by God in his treatment.

This knowledge (of the healing art) is the most important of all the sciences, for it is the greatest means from God, the Life-giver to the dust, for preserving the bodies of all people, and He has put it in the forefront of all sciences and wisdoms. For this is the day when you must arise for My Victory.

Say: Thy name is my healing, O my God, and remembrance of Thee is my remedy. Nearness to Thee is my hope, and love for Thee is my companion. Thy mercy to me is my healing and my succor in both this world and the world to come. Thou, verily, art the All-Bountiful, the All-Knowing, the All-Wise.

10

MEANS OF PRESERVING HEALTH

Be the essence of cleanliness among mankind . . . under all circumstances conform yourselves to refined manners . . . let no trace of uncleanliness appear on your clothes. . . . Immerse yourselves in pure water. . . . Verily We have desired to see in you the manifestations of Paradise on earth, so that there may be diffused from you that whereat the hearts of the favored ones shall rejoice.

11

Cleanliness and sanctity in all conditions are characteristics of pure beings and necessities of free souls. . . .

In all conditions, cleanliness and sanctity, purity and delicacy exalt humanity and make the contingent beings progress. Even when applied to physical things, delicacy causeth the attainment of spirituality, as it is established in the Holy Scriptures.

External cleanliness, although it is but a physical thing, hath a great influence upon spirituality. For example, although sound is but the vibrations of the air, which affect the tympanum of the ear, and vibrations of the air are but an accident among the accidents which depend upon the air, consider how much marvelous notes or a charming song influence the spirits! A wonderful song giveth wings to the spirit and filleth the heart with exaltation. To return to the subject, the fact of having a pure and spotless body likewise exerciseth an influence upon the spirit of man.

. . . O friends of God! Experience hath shown how much the

renouncing of tobacco, wine and opium, giveth health, strength and intellectual enjoyments, penetration of judgment and physical vigor. . . .

Therefore strive that the greatest cleanliness and sanctity, which is the great desire of 'Abdu'l-Bahá, should be resplendent among the Bahá'ís, and that the companions of God should surpass the rest of mankind in all conditions and perfections; that they may be physically and morally superior to others; that through cleanliness and purity, refinement and health, they may be the chief of wise men, and that by their affranchisement, their prudence and the control of their desires, they may be the princes of the pure, the free and the wise.   12

The drinking of wine . . . is the cause of chronic diseases, weakeneth the nerves, and consumeth the mind.   13

The powers of the sympathetic nerve are neither entirely physical nor spiritual, but are between the two. The nerve is connected with both. Its phenomena shall be perfect when its spiritual and physical relations are normal.

When the material world and the divine world are well corelated, when the hearts become heavenly and the aspirations become pure and divine, perfect connection shall take place. Then shall this power produce a perfect manifestation. Physical and spiritual diseases will then receive absolute healing.   14

I hope thou wilt become as a rising light and obtain spiritual health; and spiritual health is conducive to physical health.   15

Verily the most necessary thing is contentment under all circumstances; by this one is preserved from morbid conditions and from lassitude. Yield not to grief and sorrow; they cause the greatest misery. Jealousy consumeth the body and anger doth burn the liver; avoid these two as you would a lion.   16

SPIRITUAL HEALTH

I hope, as you have received physical health, you will receive your spiritual health. As the body will be cured of physical diseases, in the same way the spirit will be cured of all spiritual diseases. A cure of physical disease is very easy, but the cure of spiritual disease is very difficult. If one has fever and you give him medicine, the fever will vanish; but if the spirit is afflicted with the disease of ignorance, it is difficult to remove that disease. For example, if the spiritual health is afflicted with the love of the world, spiritual medicine must be given. These medicines are the advices and commands of God, which will have effect upon it. 17

I beseech God to ordain prosperity unto thee in this world, to confer favor upon thee in His supreme Kingdom, and to heal thee from the illness which has befallen thee for some hidden reason which no one knows save God. Verily, the will of God engages occasionally in some matter for which mankind is unable to find out the reason. The causes and reasons shall appear. Trust in God and confide in Him, and resign thyself to the will of God. Verily, thy God is affectionate, compassionate and merciful. He will look at thee with the glances of the eye of mercifulness, will guard thee with the eye of bounty, and will cause His mercy to descend upon thee. 18

. . . For these thy prevailing diseases are not on account of sins, but they are to make thee detest this world and know that there is no rest and composure in this temporal life.

I beg of God that thou mayest find a cheerful life . . . increase the longing . . . of the maidservants of the Merciful One and bring joy and happiness to the handmaidens of God; so that thou mayest diffuse the fragrances and chant the (revealed) verses. 19

If the health and well-being of the body be expended in the path of the Kingdom, this is very acceptable and praiseworthy; and if it is expended to the benefit of the human world in general—even though it be to their material benefit and be a means of doing good—that also is acceptable. But if the health and welfare of man be spent in sensual desires in a life on the animal plane, . . . then disease is better than such health; nay, death itself is preferable to such a life. If thou art desirous of health, wish thou health for serving the Kingdom. I hope thou mayest attain a perfect insight, an inflexible resolution, a complete health and spiritual and physical strength in order that thou mayest drink from the fountain of eternal life and be assisted by the spirit of Divine confirmation.   20

Chapter Eight

PRACTICAL APPLICATIONS OF THE SPIRITUAL LIFE

Service

THERE is no greater result than bonds of service in the Divine kingdom and attainment to the good-pleasure of the Lord. Therefore I desire that your hearts may be directed to the kingdom of God, that your intentions may be pure and sincere, your purposes turned toward altruistic accomplishment unmindful of your own welfare; nay, rather, may all your intentions center in the welfare of humanity, and may you seek to sacrifice yourselves in the pathway of devotion to mankind. Even as His Holiness Jesus Christ forfeited his life, may you likewise offer yourselves in the threshold of sacrifice for the betterment of the world; and just as His Holiness Bahá'u'lláh suffered severe ordeals and calamities nearly fifty years for you, may you be willing to undergo difficulties and withstand catastrophes for humanity in general.   1

. . . That one indeed is a man who, today, dedicateth himself to the service of the entire human race. . . .   2

O people of God! Be not occupied with yourselves. Be intent on the betterment of the world and the training of nations. The betterment of the world can be accomplished through pure and excellent deeds and well-approved and agreeable conduct.   3

The fruits of the tree of man have ever been and are goodly deeds and a praiseworthy character. Withhold not these fruits from the heedless. If they be accepted, your end is attained, and the purpose of life achieved. If not, leave them in their pastime of vain disputes. Strive, O people of God, that haply the hearts of the divers kindreds of the earth may, through the waters of your forbearance and loving-kindness, be cleansed and sanctified from animosity and hatred, and be made worthy and befitting recipients of the splendors of the Sun of Truth.   4

If thou seekest eternal glory, let thyself be humble and meek in the presence of the beloved God; make thyself the servant of all, and serve all alike. The service of the friends belongs to God, not to them. Strive to become a source of harmony, spirituality, and joyfulness to the hearts of the friends.   5

Be not idle, but active, and fear not.   6

If thou seekest after a work which is brighter and more attractive, sweeter and more delightful than all the affairs, it is the thralldom in the Threshold of the Almighty and servitude to His Highness the Lord of Might.   7

Ere long the word of God will display a wonderful influence and finally that region (America) will become the paradise of Abhá. Consequently, strive ye bravely that this aim may be accomplished in the near future. Striving means this: ye must live and move according to the Divine commands and behests, be united in loving with joy and ecstasy; . . . engage continually in the service of the Cause of God.   8

TRAINING OF CHILDREN

As to thy question concerning training children: it is incumbent upon thee to nurture them from the breast of the love of God, to urge them toward spiritual matters, to turn unto God and to acquire good manners, best characteristics and praiseworthy virtues and qualities in the world of humanity, and to study sciences with the utmost diligence; so that they may become spiritual, heavenly and attracted to the fragrances of sanctity from their childhood and be reared in a religious, spiritual and heavenly training. Verily I beg of God to confirm them therein.   9

The beloved of God and the maidservants of the Merciful must train their children with life and heart and teach them in the school of virtue and perfection. They must not be lax in this matter; they must not be inefficient. Truly, if a babe did not live at all it were better than to let it grow ignorant, for that innocent babe, in later life, would become afflicted with innumerable defects, responsible to and questioned by God, reproached and rejected by the people. What a sin this would be and what an omission!

The first duty of the beloved of God and the maid-servants of the Merciful is this: they must strive by all possible means to educate both sexes, male and female; girls like boys; there is no difference whatsoever between them. The ignorance of both is blameworthy, and negligence in both cases is reprovable. "Are they who know and they who do not know equal?"

The command is decisive concerning both. If it be considered through the eye of reality the training and culture of daughters is more necessary than that of sons, for these girls will come to the station of motherhood and will mold the lives of the children. The first trainer of the child is the mother. The babe, like unto a green and tender branch, will grow according to the way it is trained. If the training be right, it will grow right, and if crooked, the growth likewise, and unto the end of life it will conduct itself accordingly.

Hence, it is firmly established that an untrained and uneducated daughter, on becoming a mother, will be the prime factor in the deprivation, ignorance, negligence and the lack of training of many children.

O ye beloved of God and the maid-servants of the Merciful! Teaching and learning, according to the decisive texts of the Blessed Beauty (Bahá'u'lláh), is a duty. Whosoever is indifferent therein depriveth himself of the great bounty. Beware! Beware! that ye fail not in this matter. Endeavor with heart, with life, to train your children, especially the daughters. No excuse is acceptable in this matter.

Thus may eternal glory and everlasting supremacy, like unto the mid-day sun, shine forth in the assemblage of the people of

Bahá, and the heart of 'Abdu'l-Bahá become happy and thankful. 10

Teach your children what hath been revealed through the Supreme Pen. Instruct them in what hath descended from the heaven of greatness and power. Let them memorize the Tablets of the Merciful. . . . 11

PRAYERS FOR CHILDREN

O God! Educate these children. These children are the plants of Thine orchard, the flowers of Thy meadow, the roses of Thy garden. Let Thy rain fall upon them; let the Sun of Reality shine upon them with Thy love. Let Thy breeze refresh them in order that they may be trained, grow and develop and appear in the utmost beauty. Thou art the Giver! Thou art the Compassionate! 12

O unequalled Lord! For this helpless child be a protector, for this weak and sinful one be kind and forgiving.
O Creator! Although we are but useless grass, still we are of Thy garden; though we are but young trees, bare of leaves and blossoms, still we are of Thy orchard; therefore nourish this grass with the rain of Thy bounty; refresh and vivify these young, languishing trees with the breeze of Thy spiritual springtime.
Awaken us, enlighten us, sustain us, give us eternal life and accept us in Thy kingdom. 13

EDUCATION

To acquire knowledge is incumbent on all, but of those sciences which may profit the people of the earth, and not such sciences as begin in mere words, and end in mere words. The possessors of sciences and arts have a great right among the people of the world. . . . Indeed, the real treasury of man is his knowledge. Knowledge is the means of honor, prosperity, joy, gladness, happiness and exultation. 14

Now as to what thou hast asked concerning giving up the scientific attainment in Paris for the sake of confining thy days to the delivery of this Truth, it is indeed acceptable and beloved, but if thou acquire both it would be better and more perfect, because in this new century the attainment of science, arts, and *belles lettres,* whether divine or worldly, material or spiritual, is a matter which is acceptable before God and a duty which is incumbent upon us to accomplish. Therefore, never deny the spiritual things to the material, rather, both are incumbent upon thee. Nevertheless, at the time when thou art working for such a scientific attainment, thou must be controlled by the attraction of the love of thy Glorious Lord and mindful of mentioning His splendid Name. This being the case, thou must attain the art thou art studying to its perfection.   15

WORK AND WEALTH

Man should know his own self, and know those things which lead to loftiness or to baseness, to shame or to honor, to affluence or to poverty. After man has realized his own being and become mature, then for him wealth (or competence) is needed. If this wealth is acquired through a craft or profession, it is approvable.
16

In the Bahá'í Cause arts, sciences and all crafts are counted as worship. The man who makes a piece of notepaper to the best of his ability, conscientiously, concentrating all his forces on perfecting it, is giving praise to God. Briefly, all effort put forth by man from the fullness of his heart is worship, if it is prompted by the highest motives and the will to do service to humanity. This is worship: to serve mankind and to minister to the needs of the people. Service is prayer. . . .   17

True reliance is for the servant to pursue his profession and calling in this world, to hold fast unto the Lord, to seek naught but His grace, inasmuch as in His hands is the destiny of all His servants.   18

O My Servant! The best of men are they that earn a livelihood by their calling and spend upon themselves and upon their kindred for the love of God, the Lord of all worlds.   19

It behoveth thee to sever thyself from all desires save thy Lord, the Supreme, expecting no help or aid from anyone in the universe, not even from thy father or children. Resign thyself to God! Content thyself with but little of this world's goods! Verily, economy is a great treasure. If one of thy relations oppress thee, complain not against him before the magistrate; rather manifest magnificent patience during every calamity and hardship. Verily thy Master is the Lord of Faithfulness! Forgive and overlook the shortcomings which have appeared in that one, for the sake of love and affection. Know that nothing will benefit thee in this life save supplication and invocation unto God, service in His vineyard, and, with a heart full of love, (to) be in constant servitude unto Him.   20

O ye that pride yourselves on mortal riches! Know ye in truth that wealth is a mighty barrier between the seeker and his desire, the lover and his beloved. The rich, but for a few, shall in no wise attain the court of His presence nor enter the city of content and resignation. Well is it, then, with him, who, being rich, is not hindered by his riches from the eternal kingdom, nor deprived by them of imperishable dominion. By the Most Great Name! The splendor of such a wealthy man shall illuminate the dwellers of heaven, even as the sun enlightens the people of the earth!   21

They who are possessed of riches . . . must have the utmost regard for the poor, for great is the honor destined by God for those poor who are steadfast in patience. By My life! There is no honor, except what God may please to bestow, that can compare to this honor. Great is the blessedness awaiting the poor that endure patiently and conceal their sufferings, and well is it with the rich who bestow their riches on the needy and prefer them before themselves.

Please God, the poor may exert themselves and strive to earn the means of livelihood. This is a duty which, in this most great Revelation, hath been prescribed unto every one, and is accounted in the sight of God as a goodly deed. Whoso observeth this duty, the help of the invisible One shall most certainly aid him. He can enrich, through His grace, whomsoever He pleaseth. He, verily, hath power over all things. . . . 22

A PRAYER FOR THE NECESSITIES OF LIFE

Lord! Pitiful are we, grant us Thy favor; poor, bestow upon us a share from the ocean of Thy wealth; needy, do Thou satisfy us; abased, give us Thy glory. The birds of the air and the beasts of the field receive their meat each day from Thee and all beings partake of Thy care and loving-kindness.

Deprive not this feeble one of Thy wondrous grace and vouchsafe by Thy might unto this helpless soul Thy bounty.

Give us our daily bread and grant Thy increase in the necessities of life; that we may be dependent on none other but Thee, may commune wholly with Thee, may walk in Thy ways and declare Thy mysteries. Thou art the Almighty and the Loving and the Provider of all mankind. 23

GENEROSITY AND GIVING

O Ye Rich Ones on Earth! The poor in your midst are My trust; guard ye My trust, and be not intent only on your own ease. 24

. . . Blessed and happy is he that ariseth to promote the best interests of the peoples and kindreds of the earth. . . . 25

He (the true seeker) should succor the dispossessed, and never withhold his favor from the destitute. He should show kindness to animals, how much more unto his fellow-man, to him who is endowed with the power of utterance. 26

. . . God hath never burdened any soul beyond its power. . . . Whensoever he hath fulfilled the conditions implied in the verse: "Whoso maketh efforts for Us," he shall enjoy the blessings conferred by the words: "In Our Ways shall We assuredly guide him." 27

STRENGTH AND BEAUTY OF CHARACTER

I beseech Thee . . . to send down upon me from the clouds of Thy mercy that which will purify me of all that is not of Thee, that I may be worthy to praise Thee and fit to love Thee.   28

His Highness Christ has addressed the world, saying, "Except ye become as little children, ye shall in no wise enter into the Kingdom"; that is, men must become pure in heart to know God. . . . The hearts of all children are of utmost purity. They are mirrors upon which no dust has fallen. But this purity is on account of weakness and innocence, not on account of any strength and testing, for as this is the early period of their childhood their hearts and minds are unsullied by the world. They cannot display any great intelligence. They have neither hypocrisy nor deceit. This is on account of the child's weakness whereas the man becomes pure through his strength. Through the power of intelligence he becomes simple; through the great power of reason and understanding and not through the power of weakness, he becomes sincere. When he attains to the state of perfection he will receive these qualities; his heart becomes purified, his spirit enlightened, his soul is sensitized and tender; all through his great strength. This is the difference between the perfect man and the child. Both have the underlying qualities of simplicity and sincerity.   29

The source of courage and power is the promotion of the Word of God, and steadfastness in His Love.   30

O My Son! The company of the ungodly increaseth sorrow, whilst fellowship with the righteous cleaneth the rust from off the heart. He that seeketh to commune with God, let him betake himself to the companionship of His loved ones; and he that desireth to hearken unto the word of God, let him give ear to the word of His chosen ones.   31

Courtesy is, in truth, a raiment which fitteth all men, whether young or old. Well is it with him that adorneth his temple therewith, and woe unto him who is deprived of this great bounty.

    32

Whoso cleaveth to justice, can, under no circumstances, transgress the limits of moderation. . . . The civilization, so often vaunted by the learned exponents of arts and sciences, will, if allowed to overleap the bounds of moderation, bring great evil upon men. . . .   33

The essence of wisdom is the fear of God, the dread of His scourge and the apprehension of His justice and decree.   34

This fear (of God) is the chief commander of the army of thy Lord. Its hosts are a praiseworthy character and goodly deeds. Through it have the cities of men's hearts been opened throughout the ages and centuries, and the standards of ascendency and triumph raised above all other standards.   35

CHAPTER NINE

DETACHMENT AND SACRIFICE

DETACHMENT

W HEN people said to 'Abdu'l-Bahá, "We are glad, oh so glad that you are free," he replied:

"Freedom is not a matter of place, but of condition. I was happy in that prison, for those days were passed in the path of service.

To me prison was freedom.

Troubles are a rest to me.

Death is life.

To be despised is honor.

Therefore was I full of happiness all through that prison time.

When one is released from the prison of self, that is indeed freedom! For self is the greatest prison.

When this release takes place one can never be imprisoned.

Unless one accepts dire vicissitudes, not with dull resignation, but with radiant acquiescence, one cannot attain this freedom." 1

O My Servant! Free thyself from the fetters of this world, and loose thy soul from the prison of self. Seize thy chance, for it will come to thee no more. 2

O Befriended Stranger! The candle of thine heart is lighted by the hand of My power, quench it not with the contrary winds of self and passion. The healer of all thine ills is remembrance of Me, forget it not. Make My love thy treasure and cherish it even as thy very sight and life. 3

O Son of Earth! Wouldst thou have Me, seek none other than Me; and wouldst thou gaze upon My beauty, close thine eyes to the world and all that is therein; for My will and the will of another than Me, even as fire and water, cannot dwell together in one heart.

4

Detachment is as the sun; in whatsoever heart it doth shine it quencheth the fire of covetousness and self. He whose sight is illumined with the light of understanding will assuredly detach himself from the world and the vanities thereof. . . . Let not the world and its vileness grieve you. Happy is he whom riches fill not with vain-glory, nor poverty with sorrow.

5

The source of all glory is acceptance of whatsoever the Lord hath bestowed, and contentment with that which God hath ordained.

6

That seeker must at all times put his trust in God, must renounce the peoples of the earth, detach himself from the world of dust, and cleave unto Him Who is the Lord of Lords. . . .
(He) should also regard backbiting as grievous error, and keep himself aloof from its dominion, inasmuch as backbiting quencheth the light of the heart, and extinguisheth the life of the soul. He should be content with little, and be freed from all inordinate desire. He should treasure the companionship of those that have renounced the world, and regard avoidance of boastful and worldly people a precious benefit. . . . He should consume every wayward thought with the flame of His loving mention, and, with the swiftness of lightning, pass by all else save Him. . . . He should not hesitate to offer up his life for his Beloved nor allow the censure of the people to turn him away from the Truth. He should not wish for others that which he doth not wish for himself, nor promise that which he doth not fulfil.

7

The essence of detachment is for man to turn his face toward the courts of the Lord, to enter His presence, behold His countenance, and stand as witness before Him.

8

DETACHMENT NOT ASCETICISM

Disencumber yourselves of all attachment to this world and the vanities thereof. . . . Beware that ye approach them not, inasmuch as they prompt you to walk after your own lusts and covetous desires, and hinder you from entering the straight and glorious Path.

Know ye that by the world is meant your unawareness of Him Who is your Maker, and your absorption in aught else but Him. The "life to come," on the other hand signifieth the things that give you a safe approach to God, the All-Glorious, the Incomparable. Whatsoever deterreth you, in this Day, from loving God, is nothing but the world. Flee it that ye may be numbered with the blest. Should a man wish to adorn himself with the ornaments of the earth, to wear its apparels, or partake of the benefits it can bestow, no harm can befall him, if he alloweth nothing whatever to intervene between him and God, for God hath ordained every good thing, whether created in the heavens or in the earth, for such of His servants as truly believe in Him. Eat ye, O people, of the good things which God hath allowed you, and deprive not yourselves of His wondrous bounties. Render thanks and praise unto Him, and be of them that are truly thankful. 9

The pious practices of the monks and priests among the people of His Holiness the Spirit (i.e. Christ) are remembered before God; but in this Day they must abandon solitude for (the society of men), and engage in that which may profit both themselves and other men. 10

It is made incumbent on every one of you to engage in some one occupation, such as arts, trades, and the like. We have made this—your occupation—identical with the worship of God, the True One. Reflect O people, upon the mercy of God and upon His favors, then thank Him in mornings and evenings. 11

As to the fact that man must entirely forget himself, by this is meant that he should arise in the mystery of sacrifice and that is the disappearance of mortal sentiments and extinction of blamable morals which constitute the temporal gloom, and not that the physical health should be changed into weakness and debility. 12

THE MYSTERY OF SACRIFICE

The mystery of sacrifice is a most great subject and is inexhaustible.

Briefly it is as follows: The moth is a sacrifice to the candle. The spring is a sacrifice to the thirsty one. The sincere lover is a sacrifice to the loved one. The point lies in this: He must wholly forget himself. . . . He must seek the good pleasure of the True One; desire the face of the True One; and walk in the Path of the True One. . . . This is the first station of sacrifice.

The second station of sacrifice is as follows: Man must become like unto the iron thrown within the furnace of fire. The qualities of iron, such as blackness, coldness and solidity, which belong to the earth, disappear and vanish, while the characteristics of fire, such as redness, glowing and heat, which belong to the Kingdom, become apparent and visible. Therefore iron hath sacrificed its qualities and grades to the fire, acquiring the virtues of that element.

Likewise, when the souls are released from the fetters of the world, the imperfections of mankind and the animalistic darkness and have . . . partaken a share from the outpouring of the placeless and have acquired Lordly perfections, they are the "ransomed ones" of the Sun of Truth. . . .   13

It is incumbent upon thee, since thou hast attained the knowledge of God and His love, to sacrifice thy spirit and all thy conditions for the life of the world, bearing every difficulty for the comfort of the souls, sinking to the depth of the sea of ordeals for the sake of the love of faithfulness. . . .

The mystery of sacrifice is that man should sacrifice all his conditions for the divine station of God. The station of God is mercy, kindness, forgiveness, sacrifice, favor, grace and giving life to the spirits and lighting the fire of His love in the hearts and arteries.   14

. . . Nearness to God is possible through devotion to Him, through entrance into the Kingdom, and service to humanity; it is attained by unity with mankind and through loving-kindness to all; it is dependent upon investigation of truth, acquisition of praiseworthy virtues, service in the cause of Universal Peace, and personal sanctification. In a word, nearness to God necessitates sacrifice of self, severance and the giving up of all to Him. Nearness is likeness. 15

One of the requirements of faithfulness is that thou mayest sacrifice thyself and, in the divine path, close thine eye to every pleasure and strive with all thy soul that thou mayest disappear and be lost, like unto a drop, in the ocean of God's love. 16

Know thou that when the Son of Man yielded up His breath to God the whole creation wept with a great weeping. By sacrificing Himself, however, a fresh capacity was infused into all created things. Its evidences, as witnessed in all the peoples of the earth, are now manifest before thee. The deepest wisdom which the sages have uttered, the profoundest learning which any mind hath unfolded, the arts which the ablest hands have produced, the influence exerted by the most potent of rulers, are but manifestations of the quickening power released by His transcendent, His all-pervasive, and resplendent Spirit. 17

VICTORY THROUGH DETACHMENT

. . . Therefore, to-day "victory" neither hath been nor will be opposition to any one, nor strife with any person; but rather what is well-pleasing is that the cities of (men's) hearts, which are under the dominion of the hosts of selfishness and lust, should be subdued by the sword of the Word, of wisdom and of exhortation. Everyone, then, who desireth "victory" must first subdue the city of his own heart with the sword of spiritual truth and of the Word, and must protect it from remembering aught beside God: afterwards let him turn his regards towards the cities of (other's) hearts. This is what is intended by "victory": sedition hath never been nor is pleasing to God, and that which certain ignorant persons formerly wrought was never approved. *If ye be slain for His good pleasure verily it is better for you than that ye should slay.* Today the friends of God must appear in such fashion amidst (God's) servants that by their actions they may lead all unto the Lord of Glory. I swear by the Sun of the Horizon of Holiness that the friends of God never have regarded nor will regard the earth or its transitory riches.   18

O Son of Being! Thy heart is My home; sanctify it for My descent. Thy spirit is My place of revelation; cleanse it for My manifestation.   19

Be not content with the ease of a passing day, and deprive not thyself of everlasting rest. Barter not the garden of eternal delight for the dust-heap of a mortal world. Up from thy prison ascend unto the glorious meads above, and from thy mortal cage wing thy flight unto the paradise of the Placeless.   20

Blind thine eyes, that thou mayest behold My beauty; stop thine ears that thou mayest hearken unto the sweet melody of My voice; empty thyself of all learning, that thou mayest partake of My knowledge; and sanctify thyself from riches, that thou mayest obtain a lasting share from the ocean of My eternal wealth. Blind thine eyes, that is, to all save My beauty; stop thine ears to all save My word; empty thyself of all learning save the knowledge of Me; that with a clear vision, a pure heart and an attentive ear thou mayest enter the court of My holiness.   21

Man must become evanescent in God, must forget his own selfish conditions that he may thus arise to the station of sacrifice. It should be to such a degree that if he sleep, it should not be for pleasure, but to rest the body in order to do better, to speak better, to explain more beautifully, to serve the servants of God and to prove the truths. When he remains awake, he should seek to be attentive, serve the Cause of God and sacrifice his own stations for those of God. When he attains to this station, the confirmations of the Holy Spirit will surely reach him, and man with this power can withstand all who inhabit the earth.   22

Verily, I say, the world is like the vapor in a desert, which the thirsty dreameth to be water and striveth after it with all his might, until when he cometh unto it, he findeth it to be mere illusion. . . .

O my servants! Sorrow not, if, in these days and on this earthly plane, things contrary to your wishes have been ordained and manifested by God, for days of blissful joy, of heavenly delight, are assuredly in store for you. Worlds, holy and spiritually glorious, will be unveiled to your eyes. You are destined by Him, in this world and hereafter, to partake of their benefits, to share in their joys, and to obtain a portion of their sustaining grace. To each and every one of them you will no doubt attain.　　23

PRAYERS FOR DETACHMENT

O Lord, help me to be meek and lowly and strengthen me in severing myself from all things and in holding to the hem of the garment of Thy Glory, so that my heart may be filled with Thy love and leave no space for the love of the world and the attachment to its qualities. . . . Verily, Thou art merciful and, verily, Thou art the Generous, the Helper.　　24

. . . O God, my God! Look not upon my hopes and my doings, nay rather look upon Thy Will that hath encompassed the heavens and the earth.　　25

He is the Compassionate, the All-Bountiful!

O God, my God! Thou seest me, Thou knowest me; Thou art my Haven and my Refuge. None have I sought nor any will I seek save Thee, no path have I trodden nor any will I tread but the path of Thy love. In the darksome night of despair, mine eye turneth expectant and full of hope to the morn of Thy boundless favor, and at the hour of dawn my drooping soul is refreshed and strengthened in remembrance of Thy beauty and perfection. He whom the grace of Thy mercy aideth, though he be but a drop, shall become the boundless ocean, and the merest atom which the outpouring of Thy loving-kindness assisteth, shall shine even as the radiant star.

Shelter under Thy protection, O Thou Spirit of Purity, Thou Who art the All-Bountiful Provider, this enthralled, enkindled servant of Thine. Aid him in this world of being to remain steadfast and firm in Thy love and grant that this broken-winged bird may attain a refuge and shelter in Thy Divine Nest, that abideth upon the Celestial Tree.　　26

Chapter Ten

RECTITUDE AND PURITY

Deeds More Powerful Than Words

THOU hast said aright, that verily, Abdu'l-Bahá looketh to deeds and not to words. Even as it was said by Christ, "Ye shall know them by their fruits."   1

The companions of God are in this day, the lump that must leaven the peoples of the world. They must show forth such trustworthiness, such truthfulness, and perseverance, such deeds and character that all mankind may profit by their example. ... Within the very breath of such souls as are pure and sanctified far-reaching potentialities are hidden. So great are these potentialities that they exercise their influence upon all created things.   2

O army of God! Through the protection and help vouchsafed by the Blessed Beauty, ye must conduct yourselves in such a manner that ye may stand out distinguished and brilliant as the sun among other souls. Should any one of you enter a city, he should become a center of attraction by reason of his sincerity, his faithfulness and love, his honesty and fidelity, his truthfulness and loving-kindness towards all the people of the world, so that the people of that city cry out and say: "This man is unquestionably a Bahá'í, for his manners, his behavior, his conduct, his morals, his nature, and disposition reflect the attributes of the Bahá'ís.   3

Beware, O people of Bahá, lest ye walk in the ways of them whose words differ from their deeds. Strive that ye may be enabled to manifest to the peoples of the earth the signs of God, and to mirror forth His commandments. Let your acts be a guide unto all mankind, for the professions of most men, be they high or low, differ from their conduct. It is through your deeds that ye can distinguish yourselves from others. A good character is, verily, the best mantle from God. With it He adorneth the temple of His loved ones. By My life! The light of a good character surpasseth the light of the sun and the radiance thereof.

One righteous act is endowed with a potency that can so elevate the dust as to pass beyond the heaven of heavens. It can tear every bond asunder, and hath the power to restore the force that hath spent itself and vanished. . . . Be pure, O people of God, be pure; be righteous, be righteous.   4

HONESTY

Truthfulness is the foundation of all human virtues. Without truthfulness progress and success, in all the worlds of God, are impossible for any soul. When this holy attribute is established in man, all the divine qualities will also be acquired.   5

You must live and act with the utmost truthfulness, righteousness, chastity, uprightness, purity, sanctity, justice and equity. But if—I seek refuge in God—any one betray the least of trusts or neglect and be remiss in the performance of duties which are intrusted to him, or by oppression takes one penny of extortion from the subjects, or seeks after his own personal, selfish aims and ends in the attainment of his own interests, he shall undoubtedly remain deprived of the outpourings of His Highness the Almighty! Beware! Beware! lest ye fall short in that which ye are commanded in this Tablet!   6

Let truthfulness and courtesy be your adorning. Suffer not yourselves to be deprived of the robe of forbearance and justice, that the sweet savors of holiness may be wafted from your hearts upon all created things.   7

If the whole earth were to be converted into silver and gold, no man who can be said to have truly ascended into the heaven of faith and certitude would deign to regard it, much less to seize and keep it. . . . They who dwell within the tabernacle of God, and are established upon the seats of everlasting glory, will refuse though they be dying of hunger to stretch their hands, and seize unlawfully the property of their neighbor, however vile and worthless he may be.   8

Justice and Equity

. . . Be vigilant, that ye may not do injustice to anyone . . . Tread ye the path of justice, for this . . . is the straight path.   9

Be fair to yourselves and to others that the evidences of Justice may be revealed through your deeds among our faithful servants. Equity is the most fundamental among human virtues. The evaluation of all things must needs depend upon it. . . . Observe equity in your judgment, ye men of understanding heart! He that is unjust in his judgment is destitute of the characteristics that distinguish man's station.   10

The light of men is Justice, quench it not with the contrary winds of oppression and tyranny. The purpose of justice is the appearance of unity among men.   11

Know thou, of a truth, these great oppressions that have befallen the world, are preparing it for the advent of the Most Great Justice. . . .   12

The sun of Justice hath risen above the horizon of Bahá'u'lláh. For in His Tablets the foundations of such a justice have been laid as no mind hath from the beginning of creation conceived. . . .   13

Purity

Disencumber yourselves of all attachment to this world and the vanities thereof. Beware that ye approach them not, inasmuch as they prompt you to walk after your own lusts and covetous desires, and hinder you from entering the straight and glorious Path. . . . They that follow their lusts and corrupt inclinations have erred and dissipated their efforts. They indeed are of the lost.   14

O Friends! Prefer not your will to Mine, never desire that which I have not desired for you, and approach Me not with lifeless hearts defiled with worldly desires and cravings.   15

Blessed thou art and more blessed thou shalt be if thy feet be firm, thy heart tranquil through the fragrance of His Holy Spirit and thy secret and hidden thoughts pure before the Lord of Hosts.   16

The civilization so often vaunted by the learned exponents of arts and sciences, will, if allowed to overleap the bounds of moderation, bring great evil upon men. . . . If carried to excess, civilization will prove as prolific a source of evil as it had been of goodness when kept within the restraints of moderation. . . . He hath chosen out of the whole world the hearts of His servants, and made them each a seat for the revelation of His glory. Wherefore sanctify them from every defilement, that the things for which they were created may be engraven upon them.   17

O Quintessence of Passion! Put away all covetousness and seek contentment; for the covetous hath ever been deprived, and the contented hath ever been loved and praised.   18

He is not to be numbered with the people of Bahá who followeth his mundane desires, or fixeth his heart on the things of the earth. He is my true follower who, if he come to a valley of pure gold, will pass straight through it aloof as a cloud, and will neither turn back nor pause. Such a man is assuredly of Me. . . . And if he met the fairest and most comely of women, he would not feel his heart seduced by the least shadow of desire for her beauty. Such an one indeed is the creation of spotless chastity.

They that have tarnished the fair name of the Cause of God by following the things of the flesh—these are in palpable error!

Purity and chastity have been and still are, the most great ornaments for the handmaidens of God. . . . The brightness of the light of chastity sheddeth its illumination upon the worlds of the spirit. 19

The drinking of wine is . . . the cause of chronic diseases, weakeneth the nerves, and consumeth the mind. 20

Beware lest ye barter the River that is life indeed for that which the pure-hearted detest. Become ye intoxicated with the wine of the love of God, and not with that which deadeneth your minds, O ye that adore Him! 21

CHAPTER ELEVEN

OBEDIENCE AND HUMILITY

OBEDIENCE TO GOD

KNOW ye that the embodiment of liberty and its symbol is the animal. That which beseemeth man is submission unto such restraints as will protect him from his own ignorance, and guard him against the harm of the mischief-maker. Liberty causeth man to overstep the bounds of propriety, and to infringe on the dignity of his station. It debaseth him to the level of extreme depravity and wickedness.

Regard men as a flock of sheep that need a shepherd for their protection. . . .

The liberty that profiteth you is to be found nowhere except in complete servitude unto God, the Eternal Truth. Whoso hath tasted of its sweetness will refuse to barter it for all the dominion of earth and heaven.   1

The essence of religion is to testify unto that which the Lord hath revealed, and follow that which He hath ordained in His mighty Book.   2

Jesus answered them and said, "My doctrine is not mine, but His that sent me.

If any man shall do His will, he shall know of the doctrine, whether it be of God, or whether I speak of myself."   3

The first duty prescribed by God for His servants is the recognition of Him Who is the Day Spring of His Revelation and the Fountain of His laws, Who representeth the Godhead in both the Kingdom of His Cause and the world of creation.

. . . It behooveth every one who reacheth this most sublime station, this summit of transcendent glory, to observe every ordinance of Him Who is the Desire of the world. These twin duties are inseparable. Neither is acceptable without the other. Thus hath it been decreed by Him Who is the Source of Divine inspiration.

They whom God hath endued with insight will readily recognize that the precepts laid down by God constitute the highest means for the maintenance of order in the world and the security of its peoples. . . . We, verily, have commanded you to refuse the dictates of your evil passions and corrupt desires, and not to transgress the bounds which the pen of the Most High hath fixed, for these are the breath of life unto all created things. . . .

O ye peoples of the world! Know assuredly that My commandments are the lamps of My loving providence among My servants, and the keys of My mercy for My creatures. Thus hath it been sent down from the heaven of the Will of your Lord, the Lord of Revelation. Were any man to taste the sweetness of the words which the lips of the All-Merciful have willed to utter, he would, though the treasures of the earth be in his possession, renounce them one and all, that he might vindicate the truth of even one of His commandments, shining above the dayspring of His bountiful care and loving-kindness. . . .

Think not that We have revealed unto you a mere code of laws. Nay, rather, We have unsealed the choice wine with the fingers of might and power. To this beareth witness that which the Pen of Revelation hath revealed. Meditate upon this, O men of insight! 4

OBEDIENCE THROUGH FEAR AND THROUGH LOVE

Schools must first train the children in the principles of religion so that the Promise and the Threat, recorded in the Books of God, may prevent them from the things forbidden and adorn them with the mantle of the commandments. But this in such a measure that it may not injure the children by resulting in ignorant fanaticism and bigotry. 5

The people of wealth and men of honor and power must have the best possible regard for the respect of Religion. Religion is a manifest light and a strong fortress for the protection and tranquillity of the people of the world. For the fear of God commands people to do that which is just and forbids them that which is evil. If the lamp of religion remain concealed agitation and anarchy will prevail, and the orb of Justice and Equity and the sun of Peace and Tranquillity will be withheld from giving light. Every man of discernment testifies to that which is (here) mentioned. 6

O Son of Man! Neglect not My commandments if thou lovest My beauty, and forget not My counsels if thou wouldst attain My good pleasure. 7

HUMILITY

Verily, through meekness, man is elevated to the heaven of power; and again pride degrades him to the lowest station of humiliation and abasement. 8

We are all poor at His door, weak before His power, lowly at His threshold, and we possess the power of neither good nor harm. He is indeed the Confirmer, the Strengthener, the Benevolent! 9

Verily I supplicate God to confirm thee in that which He desireth, to protect thee from conceit and self-exaltation and from selfish concerns, to make thee devoted unto Him and resigned unto Him. 10

If thou art seeking everlasting glory, choose humility in the path of the True One. 11

O Son of Man! Transgress not thy limits, nor claim that which beseemeth thee not. Prostrate thyself before the countenance of thy God, the Lord of might and power. 12

O Son of Man! Humble thyself before Me that I may graciously visit thee. Arise for the triumph of My cause, that while yet on earth thou mayest obtain the victory. 13

They who are the beloved of God, in whatever place they gather and whomsoever they may meet, must evince, in their attitude towards God, and in the manner of their celebration of His praise and glory, such humility and submissiveness that every atom of the dust beneath their feet may attest the depth of their devotion. . . . They should conduct themselves in such manner that the earth upon which they tread may never be allowed to address them such words as these: "I am to be preferred above you. For witness, how patient I am in bearing the burden which the husbandman layeth upon me. I am the instrument that continually imparteth unto all beings the blessings with which He Who is the Source of all grace hath entrusted me. Notwithstanding the honor conferred upon me, the unnumbered evidences of my wealth—a wealth that supplieth the needs of all creation—behold the measure of my humility, witness with what absolute submissiveness I allow myself to be trodden beneath the feet of men. . . ."

Show forbearance and love to one another. Should any one among you be incapable of grasping a certain truth, or be striving to comprehend it, show forth, when conversing with him, a spirit of extreme kindliness and good-will. Help him to see and recognize the truth, without esteeming yourself to be, in the least, superior to him, or to be possessed of greater endowments.

The whole duty of man in this day is to attain that share of the flood of grace which God poureth forth for him. Let none, therefore, consider the largeness or smallness of the receptacle. The portion of some might lie in the palm of a man's hand, the portion of others might fill a cup, and of others even a gallon-measure. . . .

Beseech ye the one true God to grant that ye may taste the savor of such deeds as are performed in His path, and partake of the sweetness of such humility and submissiveness as are shown for His sake. 14

. . . Humility exalteth man to the heaven of glory and power, whilst pride abaseth him to the depths of wretchedness and degradation. . . . woe betide the wayward. . . . Every man of discernment, while walking upon the earth, feeleth indeed abashed, inasmuch as he is fully aware that the thing which is the source of his prosperity, his wealth, his might, his exaltation, his advancement and power is, as ordained by God, the very earth which is trodden beneath the feet of all men. There can be no doubt that whoever is cognizant of this truth, is cleansed and sanctified from all pride, arrogance, and vainglory. . . .   15

Beware that ye swell not with pride before God and disdainfully reject His loved ones. Defer ye humbly to the faithful, they that have believed in God and in His signs, whose hearts witness to His unity, whose tongues proclaim His oneness, and who speak not except by His leave. Thus do we exhort you with justice, and warn you with truth, lest perchance ye may be awakened.   16

If ye meet the abased or down-trodden, turn not away disdainfully from them, for the King of Glory ever watcheth over them and surroundeth them with such tenderness as none can fathom except them that have suffered their wishes and desires to be merged in the will of your Lord, the Gracious, the All-Wise. O ye rich ones of the earth! Flee not from the face of the poor that lieth in the dust, nay rather befriend him and suffer him to recount the tale of the woes with which God's inscrutable decree hath caused him to be afflicted. By the righteousness of God! Whilst ye consort with him, the Concourse on high will be looking upon you, will be interceding for you, will be extolling your names and glorifying your action. Blessed are the learned that pride not themselves on their attainments; and well is it with the righteous that mock not the sinful, but rather conceal their misdeeds, so that their own shortcomings may remain unveiled to men's eyes.   17

O Son of Spirit! Vaunt not thyself over the poor, for I lead him on his way and behold thee in thy evil plight and confound thee for evermore.   18

OBEDIENCE AND HUMILITY

O Son of Being! How couldst thou forget thine own fault and busy thyself with the faults of others? Whoso doeth this is accursed of Me. 19

O Son of Dust! Verily I say unto thee: Of all men the most negligent is he that disputeth idly and seeketh to advance himself over his brother. 20

He (the seeker) must never seek to exalt himself above any one, must wash away from the tablet of his heart every trace of pride and vainglory, must cling unto patience and resignation, observe silence, and refrain from idle talk. For the tongue is a smoldering fire, and excess of speech a deadly poison. Material fire consumeth the body, whereas the fire of the tongue devoureth both heart and soul. The force of the former lasteth but for a time whilst the effects of the latter endure a century. 21

The fear of God hath ever been the prime factor in the education of His creatures. Well is it with them that have attained thereunto. . . . Verily I say: The fear of God hath ever been a sure defence and a safe stronghold for all the peoples of the world. It is the chief cause of the protection of mankind, and the supreme instrument for its preservation. 22

PRAYERS FOR HUMILITY AND OBEDIENCE

I beseech Thee, O Thou who art the Lord of all names, by Thy name through which Thou hast subdued all created things, to graciously aid Thy loved ones . . . to fix their gaze at all times upon Thy pleasure, and to yield Thee thanks for the evidences of Thine irrevocable decree. For Thou art verily praiseworthy in all that Thou hast done in the past, or wilt do in the future, and art to be obeyed in whatsoever Thou hast wished or wilt wish, and to be loved in all that Thou hast desired or wilt desire. Thou lookest upon them that are dear to Thee with the eyes of Thy lovingkindness, and sendest down for them only that which will profit them through Thy grace and Thy gifts. 23

If it be Thy pleasure, make me to grow as a tender herb in the meadows of Thy grace, that the gentle winds of Thy will may stir me up and bend me into conformity with Thy pleasure, in such wise that my movement and my stillness may be wholly directed by Thee.   24

Thine is the command at all times, O Thou who art the Lord of all names and mine is resignation and willing submission to Thy will, O Creator of the heavens!   25

CHAPTER TWELVE

TESTS AND AFFLICTIONS

THOU hast questioned concerning ordeals and difficulties and catastrophes: "Are these from God or the result of man's evil deeds?"

Know thou that ordeals are of two kinds: One kind is to test the soul, and the other is punishment for actions. That which is for testing is educational and developmental and that which is the punishment of deeds is severe retribution.

The father and the teacher sometimes humor the children and sometimes discipline them. This discipline is for educational purposes and is indeed to give them true happiness; it is absolute kindness and true providence. Although in appearance it is wrath, yet in reality it is kindness. Although outwardly it is an ordeal, yet inwardly it is purifying water.

Verily, in both cases we must supplicate and implore and commune to the Divine threshold in order to be patient in ordeals. 1

Tests are benefits from God, for which we should thank Him. Grief and sorrow do not come to us by chance, they are sent to us by the Divine mercy for our own perfecting.

While a man is happy he may forget his God; but when grief comes and sorrows overwhelm him, then will he remember his Father Who is in Heaven, and Who is able to deliver him from his humiliations.

Men who suffer not, attain no perfection. The plant most pruned by the gardeners is that one which, when the summer comes, will have the most beautiful blossoms and the most abundant fruit.

The laborer cuts up the earth with his plow, and from that earth comes the rich and plentiful harvest. The more a man is chastened, the greater is the harvest of spiritual virtues shown forth by him. A soldier is no good general until he has been in the front of the fiercest battle and has received the deepest wounds. 2

Does the soul progress more through sorrow or through joy in this world?

The mind and spirit of man advance when he is tried by suffering. . . . Just as the plow furrows the earth deeply, purifying it of weeds and thistles, so suffering and tribulation free man from the petty affairs of this worldly life until he arrives at a state of complete detachment. His attitude in this world will be that of divine happiness. Man is, so to speak, unripe; the heat of the fire of suffering will mature him. Look back to the times past and you will find that the greatest men have suffered most. . . .

Through suffering (one) will attain to an eternal happiness which nothing can take from him. The Apostles of Christ suffered: they attained eternal happiness. . . .

To attain eternal happiness one must suffer. He who has reached the state of self-sacrifice has true joy. Temporal joy will vanish. 3

Thou hast written concerning the tests that have come upon thee. To the sincere ones, tests are as a gift from God, the Exalted, for a heroic person hasteneth, with the utmost joy and gladness, to the tests of a violent battlefield, but the coward is afraid and trembles and utters moaning and lamentation. Likewise, an expert student prepares and memorizes his lessons and exercises with the utmost effort, and in the day of examination he appears with infinite joy before the master. Likewise, the pure gold shines radiantly in the fire of test. Consequently, it is made clear that for holy souls, trials are as the gift of God, the Exalted; but for weak souls they are an unexpected calamity. This test is just as thou hast written; it removes the rust of egotism from the mirror of the heart until the Sun of Truth may shine therein. For no veil is greater than egotism and no matter how thin that covering may be, yet it will finally veil man entirely and prevent him from receiving a portion from the eternal bounty. 4

O Son of Man! If adversity befall thee not in My path, how canst thou walk in the ways of them that are content with My pleasure? If trials afflict thee not in thy longing to meet Me, how wilt thou attain the light in thy love for My beauty? 5

O Son of Man! My calamity is My providence, outwardly it is fire and vengeance, but inwardly it is light and mercy. Hasten thereunto that thou mayest become an eternal light and an immortal spirit. This is My command unto thee, do thou observe it. 6

Tests Distinguish the Sincere

As to trials (tests in the path of God), verily they are necessary. Hast thou not heard and read how there appeared trials from God in the days of Jesus, and thereafter, and how the whirlwind of tests became severe? Even the glorious Peter was not rescued from the flame of trials, and wavered. Then he repented and mourned the mourning of a bereaved one. . . . Is it then possible to be saved from the trials of God? No, verily. There is a great wisdom therein of which no one is aware save the wise and knowing.

Were it not for tests, genuine gold could not be distinguished from the counterfeit. Were it not for tests, the courageous could not be known from the coward. Were it not for tests, the people of faithfulness could not be known from the people of selfishness. Were it not for tests, the intellects and faculties of the scholars in the great colleges would not be developed. Were it not for tests, the sparkling gems could not be known from worthless pebbles. Were it not for tests, the fisherman could not be distinguished from Annas and Caiaphas, who had great worldly dignity.

Were it not for tests the face of Mary Magdalene would not glisten with the light of firmness and certainty unto all the horizons. These are some of the mysteries of tests which we have unfolded to thee that thou mayest become cognizant of the mysteries of God in every cycle. Verily I pray God to illumine the faces as pure gold in the fire of tests.

7

Anybody can be happy in the state of comfort, ease, health, success, pleasure and joy; but if one can be happy and contented in the time of trouble, hardship and disease, it is the proof of nobility.

8

The souls who bear the tests of God become the manifestations of great bounties; for the divine trials cause some souls to become entirely lifeless, while they cause the holy souls to ascend to the highest degree of love and firmness. They cause progress and they also cause retrogression.

9

But for tribulations, how could the assured be distinguished from the doubters among Thy servants?

10

How many the leaves which the tempests of trials have caused to fall, and how many, too, are those which, clinging tenaciously to the tree of Thy Cause, have remained unshaken by the tests that have assailed them, O Thou Who art our Lord the Most Merciful!

11

FRUITS OF TESTS AND AFFLICTIONS

Do ye not look upon the beginning of affairs; attach your hearts to the ends and results. The present period is like unto the sowing time. Undoubtedly it is impregnated with perils and difficulties, but in the future many a harvest shall be gathered, and benefits and results will become apparent. When one considers the issue and the end, inexhaustible joy and happiness will dawn.

Everything of importance in this world demands the close attention of its seeker. The one in pursuit of anything must undergo difficulties and hardships until the object in view is attained and the great success is obtained. This is the case of things pertaining to the world. How much higher is that which concerns the Supreme Concourse! That Cause involves every favor, glory and eternal bliss in the world of God.

12

As to the subject of babes and infants and weak ones who are afflicted by the hands of oppressors: this contains great wisdom and this subject is of paramount importance. In brief, for those souls there is a recompense in another world and many details are connected with this matter. For those souls that suffering is the greatest mercy of God. Verily that mercy of the Lord is far better and preferable to all the comfort of this world and the growth and development of this place of mortality. 13

Divine Assistance

Be not grieved if affairs become difficult and troubles wax intense on all sides! Verily, thy Lord changeth hardship into facility, troubles into ease and afflictions into greatest composure. 14

If thy daily living become difficult, soon (God) thy Lord will bestow upon thee that which will satisfy thee. Be patient in the time of affliction and trial, endure every difficulty and hardship with a dilated heart, attracted spirit and eloquent tongue in remembrance of the Merciful. Verily this is the life of satisfaction, the spiritual existence, heavenly repose, divine benediction and the celestial table! Soon thy Lord will extenuate thy straitened circumstances even in this world. 15

Be patient under all conditions, and place your whole trust and confidence in God. 16

Be generous in prosperity and thankful in adversity. 17

O My Servant!
Abandon not for that which perisheth an everlasting dominion, and cast not away celestial sovereignty for a worldly desire. This is the river of everlasting life that hath flowed from the well-spring of the pen of the merciful; well is it with them that drink! 18

If any one revile you, or trouble touch you, in the path of God, be patient, and put your trust in Him Who heareth, Who seeth. 19

Armed with the power of Thy name nothing can ever hurt me and with Thy love in my heart all the world's afflictions can in no wise alarm me.   20

Whosoever, O my Lord, is impatient in the tribulations befalling him in Thy path, hath not drunk of the cup of Thy love nor tasted of the sweetness of Thy remembrance.   21

Aware as I am, O my God, that Thou wilt send down upon Thy servants only what is good for them, I nevertheless beseech Thee, by Thy name which overshadoweth all things, to raise up, for their assistance and as a sign of Thy grace and as an evidence of Thy power, those who will keep them safe from all their adversaries.

Potent art Thou to do Thy pleasure. Thou art, verily, the Supreme Ruler, the Almighty, the Help in Peril, the Self-Subsisting.   22

I fear no tribulation in His path, nor any affliction in My love for Him. Verily God hath made adversity as a morning dew upon His green pasture, and a wick for His lamp which lighteth earth and heaven.   23

A PRAYER FOR PROTECTION AND PRESERVATION IN TESTS AND AFFLICTIONS

O my Lord! Thou knowest that the people are encircled with pain and calamities and are environed with hardships and troubles. Every trial doth attack man and every dire adversity doth assail him like unto the assault of a serpent. There is no shelter and asylum for him except under the wing of Thy protection, preservation, guard and custody.

O Thou the Merciful One! O my Lord! Make Thy protection my armory, Thy preservation my shield, humbleness before the door of Thy Oneness my guard, and Thy custody and defense my fortress and my abode. Preserve me from the suggestions of myself and desire and guard me from every sickness, trial, difficulty and ordeal.

Verily, Thou art the Protector, the Guardian, the Preserver, the Sufficer, and verily Thou art the Merciful of the Most Merciful!   24

How Bahá'u'lláh and 'Abdu'l-Bahá Met Afflictions

Though my body be pained by the trials that befall me from Thee, though it be afflicted by the revelations of Thy Decree, yet my soul rejoiceth at having partaken of the waters of Thy Beauty, and at having attained the shores of the ocean of Thine eternity. Doth it become a lover to flee from his beloved, or to desert the object of his heart's desire? Nay, we all believe in Thee, and eagerly hope to enter Thy presence.   25

Ye have expressed words of solicitude and anxiety over the troubles and persecutions which have befallen this imprisoned one. Do not be at all sad, be ye not affected. . . . Persecutions and adversities are merciful gifts. . . . Through the appearance of tests, my heart is consoled, and through the experiencing of dire afflictions my soul is calmed.   26

O thou friend! Be not sorrowful because of my imprisonment and lament not over my difficulties; nay, rather, ask God to increase my hardship in His path, for therein lies a wisdom which none are able to comprehend save the near angels.   27

CHAPTER THIRTEEN

LEARNING TO KNOW AND LOVE GOD

THE NECESSITY OF KNOWING AND LOVING GOD

Question.—Those who are blessed with good actions and universal benevolence, who have praiseworthy characteristics, who act with love and kindness towards all creatures, who care for the poor, and who strive to establish universal peace—what need have they of the Divine teachings? of which they think indeed that they are independent? What is the condition of these people?

Answer.—Know that such actions, such efforts, and such words are praiseworthy and approved, and are the glory of humanity. But these actions alone are not sufficient; they are a body of the greatest loveliness, but without spirit. No, that which is the cause of everlasting life, eternal honor, universal enlightenment, real salvation and prosperity, is, first of all, the knowledge of God. It is known that the knowledge of God is beyond all knowledge, and it is the greatest glory of the human world. For, in the existing knowledge of the reality of things there is material advantage, and through it outward civilization progresses; but the knowledge of God is the cause of spiritual progress and attraction, and through it the perception of truth, the exaltation of humanity, divine civilization, rightness of morals and illumination, are obtained.

Secondly, comes the love of God, the light of which shines in the lamps of the hearts of those who know God; its brilliant rays illuminate the horizon and give to man the life of the Kingdom. In truth, the fruit of human existence is the love of God, for this love is the spirit of life, and the eternal bounty. If the love of God did not exist, the hearts of men would be dead, and deprived of the sensations of existence; if the love of God did not exist, spiritual union would be lost; if the love of God did not exist, the light of unity would not illuminate humanity; if the love of God did not exist, the East and West, like two lovers would not embrace each other; if the love of God did not exist, division and disunity would not be changed into fraternity; if the love of God did not exist, indifference would not end in affection; if the love of God did not exist the stranger would not become the friend. The love of the human world has shone forth from the love of God, and has appeared by the bounty and grace of God.

It is clear that the reality of mankind is diverse, that opinions are various and sentiments different; and this difference of opinions, of thoughts, of intelligence, of sentiments among the human species, arises from essential necessity; for the differences in the degrees of existence of creatures is one of the necessities of existence, which unfolds itself in infinite forms. Therefore we have need of a general power which may dominate the sentiments, the opinions, and the thoughts of all, thanks to which these divisions may no longer have effect, and all individuals may be brought under the influence of the unity of the world of humanity. It is clear and evident that this greatest power in the human world is the love of God. It brings the different people under the shadow of the tent of affection; it gives to the antagonistic and hostile nations and families the greatest love and union.   1

There are four kinds of love. The first is the love that flows from God to man; it consists of the inexhaustible graces, the Divine effulgence and heavenly illumination. Through this love the world of being receives life. Through this love man is endowed with physical existence, until, through the breath of the Holy Spirit—this same love—he receives eternal life and becomes the image of the Living God. This love is the origin of all the love in the world of creation.

The second is the love that flows from man to God. This is

faith, attraction to the Divine, enkindlement, progress, entrance into the Kingdom of God, receiving the bounties of God, illumination with the lights of the Kingdom. This love is the origin of all philanthropy; this love causes the hearts of men to reflect the rays of the Sun of Reality.

The third is the love of God towards the Self or Identity of God. This is the transfiguration of His Beauty, the reflection of Himself in the mirror of His creation. This is the Reality of Love, the Ancient Love, the Eternal Love. Through one ray of this Love all other love exists.

The fourth is the love of man for man. The love which exists between the hearts of believers is prompted by the ideal of the unity of spirits. This love is attained through the knowledge of God, so that men see the Divine love reflected in the heart. Each sees in the other the beauty of God reflected in the soul, and, finding this point of similarity, they are attracted to one another in love. This love will make all men the waves of one sea. This love will make them all the stars of one heaven and the fruits of one tree. This love will bring the realization of true accord, the foundation of real unity.

But the love which sometimes exists between friends is not (true) love, because it is subject to transmutation; this is merely fascination. As the breeze blows, the slender trees yield. If the wind is in the east, the tree leans to the west, and if the wind is in the west, the tree leans to the east. This kind of love is originated by the accidental conditions of life. This is not love, it is merely acquaintanceship; it is subject to change.

Today you will see two souls apparently in close friendship; tomorrow all this may be changed. Yesterday they were ready to die for one another, today they shun one another's society; This is not love; it is the yielding of the hearts to the accidents of life. When that which has caused this "love" to exist passes, the love passes also; this is not in reality love.

Love is only of the four kinds I have explained. (a) The love of God towards the identity of God. Christ has said God is love. (b) The love of God for His children (for His servants). (c) The love of man for God and, (d) The love of man for man.

These four kinds of love originate from God. These are rays from the Sun of Reality; these are the breathings of the Holy Spirit; these are the signs of the Reality.   2

Having created the world and all that liveth and moveth therein, He, through the direct operation of His unconstrained and sovereign Will, chose to confer upon man the unique distinction and capacity to know Him and to love Him—a capacity that must needs be regarded as the generating impulse and the primary purpose underlying the whole of creation. . . . Upon the inmost reality of each and every created thing He hath shed the light of one of His names, and made it a recipient of one of His attributes. Upon the reality of man, however, He hath focused the radiance of all of His names and attributes, and made it a mirror of His own Self. Alone of all created things man hath been singled out for so great a favor, so enduring a bounty.   3

Is it not astonishing that although man has been created for the knowledge and love of God, for the virtues of the human world, for spirituality, heavenly illumination and life eternal, nevertheless he continues ignorant and negligent of all this? Consider how he seeks knowledge of everything except knowledge of God. For instance, his utmost desire is to penetrate the mysteries of the lowest strata of the earth. Day by day he strives to know what can be found ten meters below the surface, what he can discover within the stone, what he can learn by archaeological research in the dust. He puts forth arduous labors to fathom terrestrial mysteries, but is not at all concerned about knowing the mysteries of the Kingdom, traversing the illimitable fields of the eternal world, becoming informed of the divine realities, discovering the secrets of God, attaining the knowledge of God, witnessing the splendors of the Sun of Truth and realizing the glories of everlasting life. . . . How much he is attracted to the mysteries of matter and how completely unaware he is of the mysteries of divinity. . . . It is as if a kind and loving father had provided a library of wonderful books for his son in order that he might be informed of the mysteries of creation; at the same time surrounding him with every means of comfort and enjoyment; but the son amuses himself with pebbles and playthings, neglectful of all his father's gifts and provision. . . .

. . . Day and night you must strive that you may attain to the significances of the heavenly Kingdom, perceive the signs of Divinity, acquire certainty of knowledge and realize that this world has a Creator, a Vivifier, a Provider, an Architect—knowing this through proofs and evidences and not through susceptibilities—nay, rather through decisive arguments and real vision; that is to say, visualizing it as clearly as the outer eye beholds the sun.   4

O thou son of the Kingdom! If one possesses the love of God everything that he undertakes is useful, but if the undertaking is without the love of God, then it is hurtful and the cause of veiling oneself from the Lord of the Kingdom. But with the love of God every bitterness is changed into sweetness and every gift becometh precious. For instance, a musical and melodious voice imparteth life to an attracted heart, but lureth toward lust those souls who are engulfed in passion and desire.

With the love of God all sciences are accepted and beloved, but without it are fruitless; nay, rather, the cause of insanity. Every science is like unto a tree; if the fruit of it is the love of God, that is a blessed tree. Otherwise it is dried wood and finally a food for fire.   5

LEARNING TO KNOW GOD

(The) energies with which the Day Star of Divine bounty and source of heavenly guidance hath endowed the reality of man lie . . . latent within him even as the flame is hidden within the candle and the rays of light are potentially present in the lamp. The radiance of these energies may be obscured by worldly desires even as the light of the sun can be concealed beneath the dust and dross which cover the mirror. Neither the candle nor the lamp can be lighted through their own unaided efforts, nor can it ever be possible for the mirror to free itself from its dross. It is clear and evident that until a fire is kindled the lamp will never be ignited, and unless the dross is blotted out from the face of the mirror it can never represent the image of the sun nor reflect its light and glory.

And since there can be no tie of direct intercourse to bind the one true God with His creation, and no resemblance whatever can exist between the transient and the Eternal, the contingent and the Absolute, He hath ordained that in every age and dispensation a pure and stainless Soul be made manifest in the kingdoms of earth and heaven. . . . These Essences of Detachment, these resplendent Realities are the channels of God's all-pervasive grace. Led by the light of unfailing guidance, and invested with supreme sovereignty, they are commissioned to use the inspiration of their words, the effusions of their infallible grace and the sanctifying breeze of their Revelation for the cleansing of every longing heart and receptive spirit from the dross and dust of earthly cares and limitations. Then, and only then, will the Trust of God, latent in the reality of man, emerge, as resplendent as the rising Orb of Divine Revelation, from behind the veil of concealment, and implant the ensign of its revealed glory upon the summits of men's hearts.   6

The knowledge of the Reality of Divinity is impossible and unattainable, but the knowledge of the Manifestations of God is the knowledge of God, for the bounties, splendors, and divine attributes are apparent in them. Therefore if man attains to the knowledge of the Manifestations of God, he will attain to the knowledge of God; and if he be neglectful of the knowledge of the Holy Manifestations, he will be bereft of the knowledge of God. It is then ascertained and proved that the Holy Manifestations are the center of the bounty, signs, and perfections of God. Blessed are those who receive the light of the divine bounties from the enlightened Dawning-points.   7

He hath called into being His creatures, that they may know Him Who is the Compassionate, the All-Merciful. Unto the cities of all nations He hath sent His Messengers, Whom He hath commissioned to announce unto men tidings of the Paradise of His good pleasure, and to draw them nigh unto the Haven of abiding security, the Seat of eternal holiness and transcendent glory.   8

In the past they that were the daysprings and mines of wisdom in no wise ignored its ultimate Cause or denied its Fountain and Source. . . .

Remarkable and far-reaching as the intellectual and industrial accomplishments of the leaders of thought have been in modern times, yet to every discerning observer it is clear and manifest that they have derived the greatest part of their knowledge from the sages of the past. . . . These sages of old in their turn acquired their knowledge from the Prophets of God, for these verily were the Manifestations of Divine Wisdom and the Revealers of heavenly mysteries.   9

Immerse yourselves in the ocean of My words, that ye may unravel its secrets, and discover all the pearls of wisdom that lie hid in its depths.   10

The source of all learning is the knowledge of God, exalted be His Glory, and this cannot be attained save through the knowledge of His Divine Manifestation.   11

Ponder God in your heart, reflect on His Manifestations, and be not of them that are void of understanding.   12

Turn to God, supplicate humbly at His threshold, seeking assistance and confirmation, that God may rend asunder the veils that obscure your vision. Then will your eyes be filled with illumination, face to face you will behold the reality of God and your heart become completely purified from the dross of ignorance, reflecting the glories and bounties of the kingdom.   13

GOD'S LOVE FOR US

O Son of Man! Veiled in My immemorial being and in the ancient eternity of My essence, I knew My Love for Thee; therefore I created thee, have engraved on thee Mine image and revealed to thee My beauty.   14

What outpouring flood can compare with the stream of His all-embracing grace, and what blessing can excel the evidences of so great and pervasive a mercy? There can be no doubt whatever that if for one moment the tide of His mercy and grace were to be withheld from the world, it would completely perish. For this reason, from the beginning that hath no beginning the portals of Divine mercy have been flung open to the face of all created things, and the clouds of Truth will continue to the end that hath no end to rain on the soil of human capacity, reality and personality their favors and bounties. Such hath been God's method continued from everlasting to everlasting.   15

Thou art, in truth, He Whose mercy hath encompassed all the worlds, and whose grace hath embraced all that dwell on earth and in heaven. Who is there that hath cried after Thee, and whose prayer hath remained unanswered? Where is he to be found who hath reached forth towards Thee, and whom Thou hast failed to approach? Who is he that can claim to have fixed his gaze upon Thee, and toward whom the eye of Thy loving-kindness hath not been directed? I bear witness that Thou hast turned toward Thy servants ere they had turned toward Thee, and hadst remembered them ere they had remembered Thee. All grace is Thine, O Thou in Whose hand is the kingdom of Divine gifts and the source of every irrevocable decree.   16

. . . The manifold bounties of the Lord of all beings have, at all times, through the Manifestations of His Divine Essence, encompassed the earth and all that dwell therein. Not for a moment hath His grace been withheld, nor have the showers of His loving-kindness ceased to rain upon mankind.   17

Consider to what extent the love of God makes itself manifest. Among the signs of His love which appear in the world are the dawning-points of His Manifestations. What an infinite degree of love is reflected by the divine Manifestations toward mankind! For the sake of guiding the people they have willingly forfeited their lives to resuscitate human hearts. They have accepted the cross. To enable human souls to attain the supreme degree of advancement, they have suffered during their limited years extreme ordeals and difficulties. . . .

Observe how rarely human souls sacrifice their pleasure or comfort for others; how improbable that a man would offer his eye or suffer himself to be dismembered for the benefit of another. Yet all the divine Manifestations suffered, offered their lives and blood, sacrificed their existence, comfort and all they possessed for the sake of mankind. Therefore consider how much they love. Were it not for their love for humanity, spiritual love would be mere nomenclature. Were it not for their illumination, human souls would not be radiant. How effective is their love! This is a sign of the love of God; a ray of the Sun of Reality.   18

LEARNING TO LOVE GOD

To the heaven of Thy loving-kindness lift me up, O my Quickener, and unto the Day Star of Thy guidance lead me, O Thou my Attractor!   19

The essence of love is for man to turn his heart to the Beloved One, and sever himself from all else but God, and desire nought save that which is the desire of his Lord.   20

Help me to guard the pearls of Thy love which by Thy decree, Thou hast enshrined within my heart.   21

Let the flame of the love of God burn brightly within your radiant hearts. Feed it with the oil of Divine guidance, and protect it within the shelter of your constancy. Guard it within the globe of trust and detachment from all else but God, so that the evil whisperings of the ungodly may not extinguish its light. O My servants! My holy, My divinely ordained Revelation may be likened unto an ocean in whose depths are concealed innumerable pearls of great price, of surpassing luster. It is the duty of every seeker to bestir himself and strive to obtain the shores of this ocean, so that he may, in proportion to the eagerness of his search and the efforts he hath exerted, partake of such benefits as have been preordained in God's irrevocable and hidden Tablets.   22

Know verily nothing will benefit a person save the love of the Merciful One. Nothing illuminates a man's heart save the radiance which shines forth from the Kingdom of God! Put away every thought and doubtful mentioning and keep thy thoughts entirely on that which uplifts man to the heaven of the gift of God. . . .   23

WHAT THE LOVE OF GOD BRINGS TO US

O Son of Man! I loved thy creation, hence I created thee. Wherefore, do thou love Me that I may name thy name and fill thy soul with the spirit of life.   24

O Son of Man! Love Me that I may love thee. If thou lovest Me not, My love can in no wise reach thee. Know this, O servant.   25

O Son of Being! My love is my stronghold; he that entereth therein shall be safe and secure, and he that turneth away shall surely stray and perish.   26

O Son of Utterance! Thou art My stronghold; enter therein that thou mayest abide in safety. My love is in thee, know it, that thou mayest find Me nigh unto thee.   27

O Befriended Stranger! . . . The healer of all thine ills is remembrance of Me, forget it not. Make My love thy treasure and cherish it even as thy very sight and life.   28

The day is approaching when the intervening clouds will have been completely dissipated, when the light of the words, "All honor belongeth unto God and unto them that love Him" will have appeared, as manifest as the sun, above the horizon of the Will of the Almighty.   29

PRAYER FOR ATTAINING THE KNOWLEDGE AND THE LOVE OF GOD

O my God! O my God! This, Thy servant, hath advanced toward Thee, is passionately wandering in the desert of Thy love, walking in the path of Thy service, anticipating Thy favors, hoping for Thy bounty, relying upon Thy Kingdom, and being exhilarated with the wine of Thy gift. O my God! Increase his fervor in Thy passion, his constancy in Thy praise and his ardor in Thy love. Verily, Thou art the Beneficent and endowed with great bounty! There is no God but Thee, the Forgiving, the Merciful.   30

CHAPTER FOURTEEN

LOVE AND UNITY

THE prophets of God one and all, Christ Himself as well as the Blessed Beauty (Bahá'u'lláh), have all appeared and raised the call with the one purpose of transforming the world of man into the Kingdom of God. Their common aim was to turn the earthly into heavenly, darkness into light, things that are satanic into things Divine. They strove to establish the reign of harmony and love amongst the children of men, to unfold to their eyes the fundamental unity of all mankind, to demolish the foundations of differences in the world, and to confer upon it the imperishable blessings of eternal life.

O thou honored one! Ponder in thine heart the world of being. Association, harmony and union are the source of life, whilst differences and division are the cause of ultimate destruction. Shouldst thou reflect on all created things, thou wilt observe that the existence of every being dependeth upon the association and combination of divers elements the disintegration of which will terminate the existence of that being.

. . . This mutual helpfulness is realized either directly or through mediation, and if, for the twinkling of an eye, this confirmation and assistance does not descend upon the living being, it will become non-existent, for all the existing things are linked together and draw help from each other. Therefore the greatest foundation of the world of existence is this cooperation and mutuality.

Liken the world of existence to the temple of man. All the limbs and organs of the human body assist one another; therefore life continues. When, in this wonderful organism, there is a disconnection, life is changed to death and the parts of the body disintegrate. Likewise, among the parts of existence there is a wonderful connection and interchange of forces, which is the cause of the life of the world and the continuation of these countless phenomena. When one considers the living beings and the growing plants, he realizes that the animals and man sustain life by inhaling the emanations from the vegetable world, and this . . . element is called oxygen. The vegetable kingdom also draws life from the living creatures in the substance called carbon. In brief, the beings of sensation draw life from the growing beings and in turn the growing things receive life from the sensitive creatures. Therefore this interchange of forces and intercommunication is continued and uninterrupted.

From this illustration one can see the base of life is this mutual aid and helpfulness, and the cause of destruction and non-existence would be the interruption of this mutual assistance. The more the world aspires to civilization the more this most important matter of cooperation becomes manifest. Therefore in the world of humanity one sees this matter of helpfulness attain to a high degree of efficiency; so much so that the continuance of humanity entirely depends upon this interrelation. 1

Know thou of a certainty that Love is the secret of God's holy Dispensation, the manifestation of the All-Merciful, the fountain of spiritual outpourings. Love is heaven's kindly light, the Holy Spirit's eternal breath that vivifies the human soul. Love is the cause of God's revelation unto man, the vital bond inherent, according to Divine creation, in the realities of things. Love is the one means that insures true felicity both in this world and the next. Love is the light that guideth in darkness, the living link that uniteth God with man, that assureth the progress of every illumined soul. Love is the most great law that ruleth this mighty and heavenly Cycle, the unique power that bindeth together the divers elements of this material world, the supreme magnetic force that directs the movements of the spheres in the celestial realms. Love revealeth with unfailing and limitless power the mysteries latent in the universe. Love is the spirit of life unto the adorned body of mankind, the establisher of true civilization in this mortal world, and the shedder of imperishable glory upon every high-aiming race and nation.

Whatsoever people is graciously favored therewith by God, its name shall surely be magnified and extolled by the Concourse from on high, by the company of angels, and the denizens of the Abhá kingdom. And whatsoever people turneth its heart away from this Divine love—the revelation of the Merciful— shall err grievously, shall fall in despair, and be utterly destroyed. That people shall be denied all refuge, shall become even as the vilest creatures of the earth, victims of degradation and shame.

O ye beloved of the Lord! Strive to become the manifestations of the love of God, the lamps of Divine guidance shining amongst the kindreds of the earth with the light of love and concord. 2

LOVE AND UNITY MUST BE ALL-EMBRACING

Should any one contend that true and enduring unity can in nowise be realized in this world inasmuch as its people widely differ in their manners and habits, their tastes, their temperament and character, their thoughts and their views, to this we make reply that differences are of two kinds; the one is the cause of destruction, as exemplified by the spirit of contention and strife which animates mutually conflicting and antagonistic peoples and nations, whilst the other is the sign of diversity, the symbol and the secret of perfection, and the revealer of the bounties of the All-glorious.

. . . Consider the flowers of the garden; though differing in kind, color, form and shape, yet, inasmuch as they are refreshed by the waters of one spring, revived by the breath of one wind, invigorated by the rays of one sun, this diversity increaseth their charm and addeth unto their beauty. How unpleasing to the eye if all the flowers and plants, the leaves and blossoms, the fruit, the branches, and the trees of the garden were all of the same shape and color! Diversity of color, form and shape enricheth and adorneth the garden, and heighteneth the effect thereof. In like manner, when divers shades of thought, temperament and character, are brought together under the power and influence of one central agency, the beauty and glory of human perfection will be revealed and made manifest. Nought but the celestial potency of the Word of God, which ruleth and transcendeth the realities of all things, is capable of harmonizing the divergent thoughts, sentiments, ideas and convictions of the children of men.   3

In the estimation of God there is no distinction of color; all are one in the color and beauty of servitude to Him. Color is not important; the heart is all-important. It matters not what the exterior may be if the heart is pure and white within. God does not behold differences of hue and complexion; He looks at the hearts. He whose morals and virtues are praiseworthy is preferred in the presence of God; he who is devoted to the Kingdom is most beloved. . . .   4

When the racial elements of the American nation unite in actual fellowship and accord, the lights of the oneness of humanity will shine, the day of eternal glory and bliss will dawn, the spirit of God encompass and the Divine favors descend. Under the leadership and training of God, the real shepherd, all will be protected and preserved. He will lead them in green pastures of happiness and sustenance and they will attain to the real goal of existence. This is the blessing and benefit of unity; this is the outcome of love.   5

Every human creature is the servant of God. All have been created and reared by the power and favor of God; all have been blessed with the bounties of the same Sun of Divine truth; all have quaffed from the fountain of the infinite mercy of God; and all in His estimation and love are equal as servants. He is beneficent and kind to all. Therefore no one should glorify himself over another; no one should manifest pride or superiority toward another; no one should look upon another with scorn and contempt and no one should deprive or oppress a fellow creature. All must be considered as submerged in the ocean of God's mercy. We must associate with all humanity with gentleness and kindliness. We must love all with love of the heart.

Some are ignorant; they must be trained and educated. One is sick; he must be healed. Another is as a child; we must assist him to attain maturity. We must not detest him who is ailing, neither shun him, scorn, nor curse him; but care for him with the utmost kindness and tenderness. An infant must not be treated with disdain simply because it is an infant. Our responsibility is to train, educate and develop it in order that it may advance toward maturity. 6

I charge you all that each one of you concentrate all the thoughts of your heart on love and unity. When a thought of war comes oppose it by a stronger thought of peace. A thought of hatred must be destroyed by a more powerful thought of love. Thoughts of war bring destruction to all harmony, well-being, restfulness and content. Thoughts of love are constructive of brotherhood, peace, friendship and happiness. . . .

If you desire with all your heart friendship with every race on earth, your thought, spiritual and positive, will spread; it will become the desire of others, growing stronger and stronger, until it reaches the minds of all men. 7

When you love a member of your family or a compatriot, let it be with a ray of the Infinite Love! Let it be in God and for God! 8

MAN'S LACK OF LOVE

'Abdu'l-Bahá said:—I have just been told that there has been a terrible accident in this country. A train has fallen into the river and at least twenty people have been killed. . . . I am filled with wonder and surprise to notice what interest and excitement has been aroused throughout the whole country on account of the death of twenty people, while they remain cold and indifferent to the fact that thousands of Italians, Turks and Arabs are killed in Tripoli!* . . . Yet these unfortunate people are human beings, too.

Why is there so much interest and eager sympathy shown towards these twenty individuals, while for five thousand persons

---

* A reference to the Italo-Turkish war of 1911.

there is none? They are all men, they all belong to the family of mankind, but they are of other lands and races. It is no concern of the disinterested countries if these men are cut to pieces, this wholesale slaughter does not affect them! How unjust, how cruel this is, how utterly devoid of any good and true feeling! The people of these other lands have children and wives, mothers, daughters and little ones! In these countries today there is hardly a house free from the sound of bitter weeping, scarcely can one find a home untouched by the cruel hand of war.

Alas! we see on all sides how cruel, prejudiced and unjust is man, and how slow he is to believe in God and follow His commandments.   9

Although the body-politic is one family, yet because of the lack of symmetry some members are comfortable, and some are in the utmost misery; some members are satisfied, and some are hungry; some are clothed with the most costly garments, while some are in need of food and shelter. Why? Because this family has not that reciprocity and symmetry needed. This household is not well arranged. . . . Is it possible for a member of a family to be subjected to the utmost misery and abject poverty, and for the rest of the family to be comfortable? It is impossible, unless the rest of the family be without feeling, having become spiritually atrophied, inhospitable, unkind.   10

. . . The disease which afflicts the body-politic is lack of love and absence of altruism. In the hearts of men no real love is found, and the condition is such that unless their susceptibilities are quickened by some power so that unity, love and accord may develop within them, there can be no healing, no agreement among mankind. Love and unity are the needs of the body-politic today. Without these there can be no progress or prosperity obtained. Therefore the friends of God must adhere to the power which will create this love and unity in the hearts of the sons of men. Science cannot cure the illness of the body-politic. Science cannot create amity and fellowship in human hearts. Neither can patriotism or racial allegiance effect a remedy. It must be accomplished solely through the Divine bounties and spiritual bestowals which have descended from God in this day for that purpose. This is an exigency of the times and the Divine remedy has been provided. The spiritual teachings of the religion of God can alone create this love, unity and accord in human hearts. 11

God's Remedy

The unity which is productive of unlimited results is first a unity of mankind which recognizes that all are sheltered beneath the overshadowing glory of the All-Glorious; that all are servants of one God; for all breathe the same atmosphere, live upon the same earth, move beneath the same heavens, receive effulgence from the same sun and are under the protection of one God. This is the most great unity, and its results are lasting if mankind adheres to it; but mankind has hitherto violated it, adhering to sectarian or other limited unities such as racial, patriotic or unity of self interests; therefore no great results have been forthcoming. Nevertheless it is certain that the radiance and favors of God are encompassing, minds have developed, perceptions have become acute, sciences and arts are widespread and capacity exists for the proclamation and promulgation of the real and ultimate unity of mankind which will bring forth marvelous results. It will reconcile all religions, make warring nations loving, cause hostile kings to become friendly and bring peace and happiness to the human world. It will cement together the Orient and the Occident, remove forever the foundations of war and upraise the ensign of the Most Great Peace. These limited unities are therefore signs of that great unity which will make all the human family one by being productive of the attractions of conscience in mankind. 12

The great mass of humanity does not exercise real love and fellowship. The elect of humanity are those who live together in love and unity. They are preferable before God because the Divine attributes are already manifest in them. The Supreme Love and Unity is witnessed in the Divine Manifestations. Among them unity is indissoluble, changeless, eternal and everlasting. Each one is expressive and representative of all. If we deny one of the Manifestations of God we deny all. To inflict persecution upon one is to persecute all. In all degrees of existence each one praises and sanctifies the others. Each of them holds to the solidarity of mankind and promotes the unity of human hearts. Next to the Divine Manifestations come the believers whose characteristics are agreement, fellowship and love.   13

From the heaven of God's Will, and for the purpose of ennobling the world of being and of elevating the minds and souls of men, hath been sent down that which is the most effective instrument for the education of the whole human race. The highest essence and most perfect expression of whatsoever the peoples of old have either said or written hath, through this most potent Revelation, been sent down from the heaven of the Will of the All-Possessing, the Ever-Abiding God. Of old it hath been revealed: "Love of one's country is an element of the Faith of God." The Tongue of Grandeur hath, however, in the day of His manifestation proclaimed: "It is not his to boast who loveth his country, but it is his who loveth the world." Through the power released by these exalted words He hath lent a fresh impulse, and set a new direction, to the birds of men's hearts and hath obliterated every trace of restriction and limitation from God's holy Book. . . .   14

Though the world is encompassed with misery and distress, yet no man hath paused to reflect what the cause or source of that may be. . . . The evidences of discord and malice are apparent everywhere, though all were made for harmony and union. The Great Being saith: O well-beloved ones! The tabernacle of unity hath been raised; regard ye not one another as strangers. Ye are the fruits of one tree, and the leaves of one branch. . . .   15

If any man were to meditate on that which the Scriptures, sent down from the heaven of God's holy Will have revealed, he will readily recognize that their purpose is that all men shall be regarded as one soul. . . . If the learned and worldly wise men of this age were to allow mankind to inhale the fragrance of fellowship and love, every understanding heart would apprehend the meaning of true liberty, and discover the secret of undisturbed peace and absolute composure. 16

APPLYING THE REMEDY

When a man turns his face to God he finds sunshine everywhere. All men are his brothers. Let not conventionality cause you to seem cold and unsympathetic, when you meet strange people from other countries. Do not look at them as if you suspected them of being evil-doers, thieves and boors. You think it necessary to be very careful, not to expose yourselves to the risk of making acquaintance with such, possibly, undesirable people.

I ask you not to think only of yourselves. Be kind to the strangers, whether they come from Turkey, Japan, Persia, Russia, China or any other country in the world. Help to make them feel at home; find out where they are staying, ask if you may render them any service; try to make their lives a little happier.

In this way, even if, sometimes, what you at first suspected should be true, still go out of your way to be kind to them—this kindness will help them to become better. . . .

Let those who meet you know, without your proclaiming the fact, that you are indeed a Bahá'í.

Put into practice the teaching of Bahá'u'lláh, that of kindness to all nations. Do not be content with showing friendship in words alone; let your heart burn with loving-kindness for all who may cross your path. 17

Pray to God that thou mayest become . . . a lover of men and well-wisher of humankind. 18

Be in perfect unity. Never become angry with one another. . . . Love the creatures for the sake of God and not for themselves. You will never become angry or impatient if you love them for the sake of God. Humanity is not perfect. There are imperfections in every human being and you will always become unhappy if you look toward the people themselves. But if you look toward God you will love them and be kind to them, for the world of God is the world of perfection and complete mercy. Therefore do not look at the shortcomings of anybody; see with the sight of forgiveness. The imperfect eye beholds imperfections. The eye that covers faults looks towards the Creator of souls. He created them, trains and provides for them, endows them with capacity and life, sight and hearing; therefore they are the signs of His grandeur.   19

The great and fundamental teachings of Bahá'u'lláh are the oneness of God and unity of mankind. This is the bond of union among Bahá'ís all over the world. They become united themselves, then unite others. It is impossible to unite unless united.   20

I desire to make manifest among the friends in America a new light that they may become a new people, that a new foundation may be established and complete harmony be realized. . . . You must have infinite love for each other, each preferring the other before himself. . . . You must love your friend better than yourself; yes, be willing to sacrifice yourself. . . . I desire that you be ready to sacrifice everything for each other, even life itself; then I will know that the cause of Bahá'u'lláh has been established. . . .   21

The advent of the prophets and the revelation of the Holy Books is intended to create love between souls and friendship between the inhabitants of the earth. Real love is impossible unless one turn his face towards God and be attracted to His beauty.   22

Be most loving one to another. Burn away, wholly for the sake of the Well-Beloved, the veil of self with the flame of the undying Fire, and with faces, joyous and beaming with light, associate with your neighbor.   23

Consort with all men, O people of Bahá, in a spirit of friendliness and fellowship. If ye be aware of a certain truth, if ye possess a jewel, of which others are deprived, share it with them in a language of utmost kindliness and good-will. If it be accepted, if it fulfill its purpose, your object is attained. If anyone should refuse it, leave him unto himself, and beseech God to guide him. Beware lest ye deal unkindly with him. A kindly tongue is the lodestone of the hearts of men. It is the bread of the spirit, it clotheth the words with meaning, it is the fountain of the light of wisdom and understanding.   24

Consort with the peoples of religions with joy and fragrance; . . . The followers of sincerity and faithfulness must consort with all the people of the world with joy and fragrance; for association is always conducive to union and harmony, and union and harmony are the cause of the order of the world and the life of the nations. Blessed are they who hold fast to the rope of compassion and kindness and are detached from animosity and hatred!   25

When you meet those whose opinions differ from your own, do not turn your face from them. . . .
Do not allow difference of opinion, or diversity of thought to separate you from your fellow-men, or to be the cause of dispute, hatred and strife in your hearts.   26

. . . Blessed is he who is illumined with the light of courtesy, and is adorned with the mantle of uprightness! He who is endowed with courtesy is endowed with a great station. . . .   27

O Son of Man! If thou lookest toward mercy, regard not that which benefits thee, and hold to that which will benefit the servants. If thou lookest toward justice, choose thou for others what thou choosest for thyself.   28

This is the Day whereon the ocean of God's mercy hath been manifested unto men, the Day in which the Day Star of His loving-kindness hath shed its radiance upon them, the Day in which the clouds of His bountiful favor have overshadowed the whole of mankind. Now is the time to cheer and refresh the down-cast through the invigorating breeze of love and fellow-ship, and the living waters of friendliness and charity.   29

O ye friends of God! Show ye an endeavor that all the nations and communities of the world, even the enemies, put their trust, assurance and hope in you; that if a person falls into error for a hundred thousand times he may yet turn his face to you hopeful that you will forgive his sins; for he must not become hopeless, neither grieved nor despondent! This is the conduct of the people of Bahá!   30

O ye beloved of the Lord! In this sacred Dispensation, conflict and contention are in no wise permitted. Every aggressor deprives himself of God's grace. It is incumbent upon everyone to show the utmost love, rectitude of conduct, straightforwardness and sincere kindliness unto all the peoples and kindreds of the world, be they friends or strangers. So intense must be the spirit of love and loving-kindness, that the stranger may find himself a friend, the enemy a true brother, no difference whatsoever existing between them. For universality is of God and all limitations earthly. Thus man must strive that his reality may manifest virtues and perfections, the light whereof may shine upon everyone. The light of the sun shineth upon all the world and the merciful showers of Divine Providence fall upon all peoples. The vivifying breeze reviveth every living creature and all beings endued with life obtain their share and portion at His heavenly board. In like manner, the affections and loving-kindness of the servants of the One True God must be bountifully and universally extended to all mankind. Regarding this, restrictions and limitations are in no wise permitted.

Wherefore, O my loving friends! Consort with all the peoples, kindreds and religions of the world with the utmost truthfulness, uprightness, faithfulness, kindliness, good-will and friendliness. . . .   31

Warnings and Promises

. . . Act in such a way that your heart may be free from hatred. Let not your heart be offended with any one. If someone commits an error and wrong toward you, you must instantly forgive him. Do not complain of others. Refrain from reprimanding them, and if you wish to give admonition or advice let it be offered in such a way that it will not burden the receiver. 32

Beware lest ye offend any heart, lest ye speak against any one in his absence, lest ye estrange yourselves from the servants of God. You must consider all His servants as your own family and relations. Direct your whole effort towards the happiness of those who are despondent, bestow food upon the hungry, clothe the needy and glorify the humble. Be a helper to every helpless one, and manifest kindness to your fellow creatures in order that you may attain the good pleasure of God. 33

Should ye attribute a mistake to a person, it will be a cause of offense and grief to him—how much greater would this be if it is attributed to a number of people! How often it hath occurred that a slight difference hath caused a great dissension and hath been made a reason for division. 34

Self-love is a strange trait and the means of destruction of many important souls in the world. If man be imbued with all good qualities but be selfish, all the other virtues will fade or pass away and eventually he will grow worse. 35

It hath been decided by the Desire of God that union and harmony may day by day increase among the friends of God and the maid-servants of the Merciful One in the West. Not until this is realized will the affairs advance by any means whatever! And the greatest means for the union and harmony of all is spiritual meetings. This matter is very important and is as a magnet (to attract) Divine confirmation. 36

When a man ariseth to expound the arguments of God and to invite people to enter the religion of God, . . . and advanceth consummate proofs concerning the appearance of the great Kingdom, then intense love shall become manifest in his heart. This love causeth the development of his spirit by the grace of the beneficent Lord. 37

Souls are liable to estrangement. Such methods should be adopted that the estrangement should be first removed, then the Word will have effect. 38

O My servant! Purge thy heart from malice and, innocent of envy, enter the divine court of holiness. 39

O son of being! Ascribe not to any soul that which thou wouldst not have ascribed to thee, and say not that which thou doest not. This is My command to thee, do thou observe it. 40

O ye beloved of the Lord! Commit not that which defileth the limpid stream of love or destroyeth the sweet fragrance of friendship. By the righteousness of the Lord! ye were created to show love one to another and not perversity and rancor. Take pride not in love for yourselves but in love for your fellow creatures. 41

PRAYERS FOR LOVE AND UNITY

O Thou kind Lord! Thou hast created all humanity from the same stock. Thou hast decreed that all shall belong to the same household. In Thy Holy Presence they are all Thy servants, and all mankind are sheltered beneath Thy Tabernacle; all have gathered together at Thy Table of Bounty; all are illumined through the light of Thy Providence.

O God! Thou art kind to all, Thou hast provided for all, dost shelter all, conferrest life upon all, Thou hast endowed each and all with talents and faculties, and all are submerged in the Ocean of Thy Mercy.

O Thou kind Lord! Unite all. Let the religions agree and make the nations one, so that they may see each other as one family and the whole earth as one home. May they all live together in perfect harmony.

O God! Raise aloft the banner of the oneness of mankind.

Cement Thou, O God, the hearts together.

O Thou kind Father, O God! Gladden our hearts through the fragrance of Thy love. Brighten our eyes through the Light of Thy Guidance. Delight our ears with the melody of Thy Word, and shelter us all in the Stronghold of Thy Providence.

Thou art the Mighty and Powerful, Thou art the Forgiving and Thou art the One who overlookest the shortcomings of all mankind! 42

O kind Lord! Thou Who art generous and merciful! We are the servants of Thy threshold and we are under the protection of Thy mercy. The Sun of Thy providence is shining upon all and the clouds of Thy mercy shower upon all. Thy gifts encompass all, Thy providence sustains all, Thy protection overshadows all and the glances of Thy favor illumine all. O Lord! Grant unto us Thine infinite bestowals and let the light of Thy guidance shine. Illumine the eyes, make joyous the souls and confer a new spirit upon the hearts. Give them eternal life. Open the doors of Thy knowledge; let the light of faith shine. Unite and bring mankind into one shelter beneath the banner of Thy protection, so that they may become as waves of one sea, as leaves and branches of one tree, and may assemble beneath the shadow of the same tent. May they drink from the same fountain. May they be refreshed by the same breezes. May they obtain illumination from the same source of light and life. Thou art the Giver, the Merciful! 43

Chapter Fifteen

ETERNAL LIFE

What Is Eternal Life?

THE immortality of the spirit is mentioned in the Holy Books; it is the fundamental basis of the divine religions. Now punishments and rewards are said to be of two kinds. First, the rewards and punishments of this life; secondly, those of the other world. But the paradise and hell of existence are found in all the worlds of God, whether in this world or in the spiritual heavenly worlds. Gaining these rewards is the gaining of eternal life. That is why Christ said, "Act in such a way that you may find eternal life, and that you may be born of water and the spirit, so that you may enter into the Kingdom."

. . . The rewards of the other world are the eternal life which is clearly mentioned in all the Holy Books, the divine perfections, the eternal bounties, and everlasting felicity. The rewards of the other world are the perfections and the peace obtained in the spiritual worlds after leaving this world; whilst the rewards of this life are the real luminous perfections which are realized in this world, and which are the cause of eternal life, for they are the very progress of existence. It is like the man who passes from the embryonic world to the state of maturity, and becomes the manifestation of these words: "Blessed be God, the best of Creators." The rewards of the other world are peace, the spiritual graces, the various spiritual gifts in the Kingdom of God, the gaining of the desires of the heart and the soul, and the meeting of God, in the world of eternity. In the same way the punishments of the other world, that is to say, the torments of the

other world, consist in being deprived of the special divine blessings and the absolute bounties, and falling into the lowest degrees of existence. He who is deprived of these divine favors,
although he continues after death, is considered as dead by the
people of truth.   1

Thou hast asked me concerning the nature of the soul. Know,
verily, that the soul is a sign of God, a heavenly gem whose
reality the most learned of men have failed to grasp, and whose
mystery no mind, however acute, can ever hope to unravel. It
is the first among all created things to declare the excellence of
its Creator, the first to recognize His glory, to cleave to His truth,
and to bow down in adoration before Him. If it be faithful to
God, it will reflect His light, and will, eventually, return unto
Him. If it fail, however, in its allegiance to its Creator, it will
become a victim to self and passion, and will, in the end, sink
in their depths.   2

DEATH IS CHANGE OF CONDITION

. . . If the body undergoes a change, the spirit need not be
touched. When you break a glass on which the sun shines, the
glass is broken, but the sun still shines! . . . If a lamp is broken,
the flame can still burn bright!

The same thing applies to the spirit of man. Though death
destroys his body, it has no power over the spirit—this is eternal,
everlasting. . . .   3

. . . To consider that after the death of the body the spirit
perishes, is like imagining that a bird in a cage will be destroyed
if the cage is broken, though the bird has nothing to fear from
the destruction of the cage. Our body is like the cage and the
spirit is like the bird. We see that without the cage this bird
flies in the world of sleep; therefore if the cage becomes broken,
the bird will continue and exist; its feeling will be even more
powerful, its perceptions greater, and its happiness increased.   4

A friend asked: "How should one look forward to death?"
'Abdu'l-Bahá answered: "How does one look forward to the end

of any journey? With hope and with expectation. It is even so with the end of this earthly journey. In the next world man will find himself freed from many of the disabilities under which he now suffers. Those who have passed on through death, have a sphere of their own. It is not removed from ours: their work of the Kingdom, is ours; but it is sanctified from what we call time and place. Time with us is measured by the sun. When there is no more sunrise, and no more sunset, that kind of time does not exist for man. Those who have ascended have different attributes (conditions) from those who are still on earth, yet there is no real separation.

"In prayer there is a mingling of stations, a mingling of condition. Pray for them as they pray for you."   5

LIFE AFTER DEATH

The mysteries of which man is heedless in this earthly world, those will he discover in the heavenly world, and there will he be informed of the secret of truth; how much more will he recognize or discover persons with whom he hath been associated. Undoubtedly, the holy souls who find a pure eye and are favored with insight will, in the kingdom of lights, be acquainted with all mysteries, and will seek the bounty of witnessing the reality of every great soul. Even they will manifestly behold the Beauty of God in that world. Likewise will they find all the friends of God, both those of the former and recent times, present in the heavenly assemblage.

As to the difference and distinction between Lazarus and that "rich man": the first was spiritual, while the second was material. One was in the highest degree of knowledge and the other in the lowest depths of ignorance. The difference and distinction will naturally become realized between all men after their departure from this mortal world. But this (distinction) is not in respect to place, but it is in respect to the soul and conscience. For the Kingdom of God is sanctified (or free) from time and place; it is another world and another universe. But the holy souls are promised the gift of intercession. And know thou for a certainty, that in the divine worlds, the spiritual beloved ones (believers) will recognize each other, and will seek union (with each other), but a spiritual union. Likewise, a love that one may have entertained for any one will not be forgotten in the world of the Kingdom. Likewise, thou wilt not forget (there) the life that thou hast had in the material world.   6

Death proffereth unto every confident believer the cup that is life indeed. It bestoweth joy, and is the bearer of gladness. It conferreth the gift of everlasting life.   7

O Son of the Supreme!
I have made death a messenger of joy to thee. Wherefore dost thou grieve? I made the light to shed on thee its splendor. Why dost thou veil thyself therefrom?   8

It is clear and evident that all men shall, after their physical death, estimate the worth of their deeds, and realize all that their hands have wrought. . . . They that are the followers of the one true God, shall, the moment they depart out of this life, experience such joy and gladness as would be impossible to describe, while they that live in error shall be seized with such fear and trembling, and shall be filled with such consternation, as nothing can exceed. Well is it with him that hath quaffed the choice and incorruptible wine of faith through the gracious favor and the manifold bounties of Him Who is the Lord of all Faiths. . . .   9

How often hath a sinner attained, at the hour of death, to the essence of faith, and, quaffing the immortal draught, hath taken his flight unto the Concourse on high!   10

It is evident that the loftiest mansions in the Realm of Immortality have been ordained as the habitation of them that have truly believed in God and in His signs. Death can never invade that holy seat.   11

Know thou, of a truth, that if the soul of man hath walked in the ways of God, it will, assuredly, return and be gathered to the glory of the Beloved. . . . It shall attain a station such as no pen can depict, or tongue describe. The soul that hath remained faithful to the Cause of God, and stood unwaveringly firm in His Path shall, after his ascension, be possessed of such power that all the worlds which the Almighty hath created can benefit through him. Such a soul provideth, at the bidding of the Ideal King and Divine Educator, the pure leaven that leaveneth the world of being, and furnisheth the power through which the arts and wonders of the world are made manifest. Consider how meal needeth leaven to be leavened with. Those souls that are the symbols of detachment are the leaven of the world. Meditate on this, and be of the thankful.   12

It is possible that the condition of those who have died in sin and unbelief may become changed; that is to say, they may become the object of pardon through the bounty of God, not through His justice; for bounty is giving without desert, and justice is giving what is deserved. As we have power to pray for these souls here, so likewise we shall possess the same power in the other world, which is the Kingdom of God. Are not all the people in the world the creatures of God? In that world also they can make progress. As here they can receive light by their supplications, there also they can plead for forgiveness, and receive light through entreaties and supplications. Thus as souls in this world, through the help of the supplications, the entreaties, and the prayers of the holy ones, can acquire development, so is it the same after death. Through their own prayers they can also progress; more especially when they are the object of the intercession of the Holy Manifestations.   13

CONSOLATION FOR THE BEREAVED

From the death of that beloved youth, due to his separation from you the utmost sorrow and grief has been occasioned, for he flew away in the flower of his age and the bloom of his youth, to the heavenly nest.

But as he has been freed from this sorrow-stricken shelter and has turned his face toward the everlasting nest of the Kingdom and has been delivered from a dark and narrow world and has

hastened to the sanctified realm of Light, therein lies the consolation of our hearts.

The inscrutable divine wisdom underlies such heart-rending
occurrences. It is as if a kind gardener transfers a fresh and
tender shrub from a narrow place to a vast region. This trans-
ference is not the cause of the withering, the waning or the
destruction of that shrub, nay, rather, it makes it grow and
thrive, acquire freshness and delicacy, and attain verdure and
fruition. This hidden secret is well-known to the gardener,
while those souls who are unaware of this bounty suppose that
the gardener in his anger and wrath has uprooted the shrub.
But to those who are aware this concealed fact is manifest and
this predestined decree considered a favor. Do not feel grieved
and disconsolate therefore at the ascension of that bird of faithfulness, nay under all circumstances pray and beg for that youth
forgiveness and elevation of station.

I hope that you will attain to the utmost patience, composure
and resignation, and I supplicate and entreat at the threshold of
Oneness and beg pardon and forgiveness. My hope from the
infinite bounties of God is that He may cause this dove of the
garden of faith to abide on the branch of the Supreme Concourse
that it may sing in the best of tunes the praises and the excel-
lences of the Lord of names and attributes.   14

PRAYERS FOR THE DEPARTED

O my God! O Thou Forgiver of sins! Bestower of Gifts!
Dispeller of afflictions!

Verily I beseech Thee to forgive the sins of such as have aban-
doned the physical garment and hastened to the spiritual world.

O my Lord! Purify them from trespasses, dispel their sorrows
and change their darkness into light. Cause them to enter the
Garden of Happiness, cleanse them with the most pure water
and grant them to behold Thy splendors on the Loftiest Mount.
                                                           15

O Thou forgiving Lord! Although certain souls finished the
days of life in ignorance, were estranged and selfish, yet the ocean

of Thy forgiveness is, verily, able to redeem and make free the sinners by one of its waves. Thou redeemest whomsoever Thou willest and deprivest whomsoever Thou willest not! Shouldst Thou treat justly, we all are sinners and deserve to be deprived; and shouldst Thou observe mercy, every sinner shall be made pure and every stranger shall become a friend. Therefore forgive and pardon and grant Thy mercy unto all. Thou art the Forgiver, the Light-Giver, and the Compassionate! 16

REFERENCE NOTES

ABBREVIATIONS USED

ABL	'Abdu'l-Bahá in London
ADJ	The Advent of Divine Justice
BNE	Bahá'u'lláh and the New Era
BP	Bahá'í Prayers (1954 edition)
BW	The Bahá'í World
BWF	Bahá'í World Faith
ESW	Epistle to the Son of the Wolf
GL	Gleanings from the Writings of Bahá'u'lláh
HW	The Hidden Words of Bahá'u'lláh
IQ	The Kitáb-i-Íqán (The Book of Certitude)
P&M	Prayers and Meditations
PUP	The Promulgation of Universal Peace
SAQ	Some Answered Questions
SDC	The Secret of Divine Civilization
SV	The Seven Valleys and the Four Valleys
TAB	Tablets of 'Abdu'l-Bahá—I, II, III
TAB-SW	Tablets of 'Abdu'l-Bahá, published only in Star of the West
TN	A Traveller's Narrative
WAB	The Wisdom of 'Abdu'l-Bahá (Paris Talks, British edition)
WOB	The World Order of Bahá'u'lláh

REFERENCE NOTES

Chapter One—TRUST IN GOD

1. Luke 12:6, 7. 2. WAB 99. 3. TAB 190. 4. TAB 200. 5. TAB 557. 6. TAB 170. 7. TAB 158. 8. ESW 76. 9. BWF 140. 10. WAB 101. 11. TAB 177. 12. TAB 381. 13. TAB 455. 14. TAB 337, 338. 15. PUP 45, 46. 16. P&M 236. 17. P&M 113, 114. 18. P&M 250. 19. P&M 212. 20. P&M 245, 246. 21. PUP 463.

Chapter Two—ENTRANCE INTO THE KINGDOM OF GOD

1. John 3:3, 5, 6. 2. BWF 261. 3. TAB 604, 605. 4. SAQ 282. 5. WAB 155. 6. PUP 220. 7. TAB 673, 674, 263, WAB 102. 8. TAB 709, 710. 9. (*). 10. TAB-SW. 11. HW 12. 12. TAB 405. 13. PUP 220, 221. 14. BP 95, 96.

Chapter Three—ADVANCING TOWARD THE IMMORTAL REALM

1. HW 24. 2. HW 3, 4. 3. BWF 229. 4. TAB 206. 5. HW 11. 6. GL 196. 7. BW vol. 1, 43. 8. SDC 4, 19, 23, 24. 9. BWF 389, 390. 10. P&M 314. 11. GL 70. 12. PUP 66, 67. 13. SAQ 273, 274. 14. BW vol. 1, 12. 15. BP 29.

Chapter Four—PRAYER AND MEDITATION

1. TAB-SW. 2. TAB 683, 684. 3. TAB 3. 4. TAB 69. 5. GL 280. 6. TAB 98. 7. ESW 94. 8. GL 323. 9. HW 8. 10. WAB 155. 11. HW 18. 12. TAB 89, 90. 13. GL 291. 14. TAB 639. 15. TAB 522. 16. P&M 283. 17. BP 108-110. 18. BP 106, 107. 19. WAB 45. 20. TAB 168. 21. WAB 55. 22. TAB 247. 23. WAB 86, 87. 24. P&M 312. 25. PUP 241, 242. 26. SV 22. 27. P&M 249, 250. 28. WAB 73. 29. BWF 359. 30. GL 265. 31. TAB 186. 32. TAB 694, 695. 33. WAB 105-107. 34. GL 266. 35. TAB 277. 36. GL 243. 37. TAB 113. 38. TAB 661. 39. TAB-SW. 40. SAQ 268. 41. PUP 182, 183.

42. TAB 483. 43. TAB 426. 44. TAB 484. 45. GL 303. 46. HW 13. 47. P&M 240. 48. P&M 90. 49. P&M 315. 50. P&M 117. 51. GL 295. 52. P&M 103, 104. 53. P&M 272. 54. P&M 105. 55. P&M 329-332. 56. IQ 238. 57. WAB 163, 164. 58. PUP 454-456. 59. BNE 114, 115. 60. GL 136.

Chapter Five—THE POWER OF THE HOLY SPIRIT

1. SAQ 165, 166. 2. WAB 51-53. 3. SAQ 146. 4. PUP 282. 5. PUP 243, 244. 6. PUP 271. 7. WAB 153, 154. 8. TAB 193. 9. TAB 343. 10. TAB 705. 11. TAB 274. 12. TAB 601. 13. BWF 369.

Chapter Six—FAITH AND CERTITUDE

1. WOB 109. 2. P&M 323. 3. TAB 549. 4. GL 86, 87. 5. Hebrews 11:1-38, 12:1. 6. IQ 222-224. 7. BWF 141. 8. GL 141. 9. WOB 107. 10. PUP 331. 11. TAB 71, 72. 12. TAB 62. 13. BP 131. 14. GL 143. 15. TAB 168. 16. IQ 195, 196; GL 267. 17. TAB 166. 18. TAB 234. 19. GL 105, 106. 20. BWF 188.

Chapter Seven—HEALING and HEALTH

1. BWF 375, 376. 2. BNE 131. 3. SAQ 296-298. 4. SAQ 294, 295. 5. WAB 100. 6. WAB 15. 7. WAB 16. 8. TAB 628, 629. 9. PUP 241. 10. BNE 137, 138. 11. BNE 127. 12. TAB 581, 582, 585. 13. ADJ 27. 14. TAB 309. 15. TAB 305, 306. 16. BNE 133. 17. TAB-SW. 18. Idem. 19. TAB 185, 186. 20. BWF 376.

Chapter Eight—PRACTICAL APPLICA-TIONS OF THE SPIRITUAL LIFE

1. PUP 51, 52. 2. GL 250. 3. BWF 174. 4. ESW 26. 5. TAB 61, 62. 6. TAB 162. 7. TAB 658. 8. TAB 511. 9. BWF 383. 10. TAB 579, 580. 11. BNE 188. 12. BP 16, 17. 13. TAB 588. 14. BWF 189.

15. BWF 376, 377. 16. BWF 167. 17. WAB 164, 165. 18. BWF 141. 19. HW 51. 20. BWF 374, 375. 21. HW 41. 22. BWF 130, 131. 23. BP 12, 13. 24. HW 41. 25. GL 250. 26. IQ 194. 27. BWF 35, 106, 107. 28. BWF 144. 29. PUP 50. 30. BWF 141. 31. HW 42. 32. ESW 50. 33. GL 342. 34. BWF 140. 35. ESW 136.

Chapter Nine—DETACHMENT AND SACRIFICE

1. BW vol. 4, 384. 2. HW 36. 3. HW 33. 4. Idem. 5. BW vol. 1, 42. 6. BWF 140. 7. IQ 193, 194. 8. BWF 141. 9. GL 276. 10. BWF 193. 11. BWF 195. 12. TAB 244. 13. TAB 354, 355. 14. TAB 65. 15. PUP 143. 16. TAB 552. 17. GL 85, 86. 18. TN 114, 115. 19. HW 17. 20. HW 36. 21. HW 25. 22. BWF 384. 23. GL 328, 329. 24. BP 81. 25. P&M 318. 26.BP 107, 108.

Chapter Ten—RECTITUDE AND PURITY

1. TAB 311. 2. ADJ 19. 3. ADJ 21. 4. ADJ 21, 20. 5. BWF 384. 6. TAB 403, 404. 7. GL 305. 8. ADJ 19, 20. 9. BWF 40. 10. ADJ 20, 21. 11. ADJ 23. 12. Idem. 13. ADJ 24. 14. ADJ 26, 27. 15. HW 28. 16. TAB 704. 17. ADJ 26. 18. HW 39. 19. ADJ 26, 27. 20. ADJ 27. 21. Idem.

Chapter Eleven—OBEDIENCE AND HUMILITY

1. GL 335, 336. 2. BWF 140. 3. John 7:16, 17. 4. GL 330-333. 5. BWF 182. 6. BWF 198. 7. HW 13. 8. BWF 180. 9. TAB 314, 315. 10. TAB 137. 11. TAB 214. 12. HW 9. 13. HW 13. 14. GL 7-9. 15. ESW 30, 44. 16. GL 128. 17. GL 314, 315. 18. HW 10. 19. Idem. 20. HW 23, 24. 21. IQ 193. 22. ESW 27. 23. P&M 238, 239. 24. P&M 240. 25. P&M 320.

Chapter Twelve—TESTS AND AFFLICTIONS

1. TAB-SW. 2. WAB 45. 3. WAB 166, 167. 4. TAB 722, 723. 5. HW 15. 6. Idem. 7. TAB-SW. 8. BWF 363. 9. TAB 324.

10. P&M 9. 11. P&M 77. 12. TAB 265, 266. 13. BWF 372. 14. TAB 311. 15. TAB 98. 16. GL 296. 17. GL 285. 18. HW 35. 19. ESW 24. 20. P&M 208. 21. P&M 136. 22. P&M 23. 23. ESW 17. 24. BF 66, 67. 25. P&M 96. 26. TAB-SW. 27. TAB 333.

Chapter Thirteen—LEARNING TO KNOW AND LOVE GOD

1. SAQ 344-346. 2. WAB 168, 169. 3. GL 65. 4. PUP 221, 222. 5. BWF 366. 6. GL 65-67. 7. SAQ 257, 258. 8. GL 144, 145. 9. BW vol. 4, 104. 10. GL 136. 11. BWF 141. 12. BW vol. 2, 62. 13. PUP 287. 14. HW 4. 15. GL 68, 69. 16. P&M 254. 17. GL 18. 18. PUP 250, 251. 19. P&M 259. 20. BWF 140, 141. 21. P&M 176. 22. GL 325, 326. 23. TAB 53. 24. HW 4. 25. Idem. 26. HW 5. 27. HW 6. 28. HW 33. 29. GL 306. 30. BP 82.

Chapter Fourteen—LOVE AND UNITY

1. BW vol. 2, 50; TAB-SW. 2. BW vol. 2, 50. 3. BW vol. 2, 54, 55. 4. PUP 41, 42. 5. PUP 54. 6. PUP 60. 7. WAB 24, 25. 8. WAB 33. 9. WAB 105, 106. 10. (*). 11. PUP 166. 12. BWF 257, 258. 13. PUP 203. 14. GL 95, 96. 15. GL 218. 16. GL 260. 17. WAB 11, 12. 18. TAB 546. 19. PUP 89. 20. PUP 150. 21. PUP 213. 22. TAB 505. 23. GL 316. 24. GL 289. 25. BWF 168. 26. WAB 47. 27. BWF 175. 28. BWF 180. 29. BWF 124. 30. TAB 436. 31. BWF 445. 32. PUP 448, 449. 33. PUP 465. 34. TAB 21. 35. TAB 136. 36. TAB 124, 125. 37. TAB 681, 682. 38. TAB 391. 39. HW 36. 40. HW 10. 41. BW vol. 2, 55. 42. BP 45. 43. BP 43, 44.

Chapter Fifteen—ETERNAL LIFE

1. SAQ 259-261. 2. BWF 121. 3. WAB 59. 4. SAQ 264. 5. ABL 97. 6. TAB 205, 206. 7. GL 345. 8. HW 11. 9. GL 171. 10. GL 266. 11. GL 141. 12. GL 161. 13. SAQ 269. 14. BWF 379, 380. 15. BP 23. 16. TAB 178, 179.

(*) Unpublished address of 'Abdu'l-Bahá in Montreal, September 3, 1912